Creative Chaos

The surprising mystery of time, self, and meaning.

ANDRE RABE

Published in 2019 by Andre Rabe Publishing

© Andre Rabe, 2019

ISBN 978-0-9931554-2-0

TABLE OF CONTENTS

Acknowledgements

To put one's intuitions into words is a most rewarding exercise but also unexpectedly difficult. Subtle contradictions and inconsistencies only come to light when we try to find language for these impressions. But new insights and greater clarity are rewards that are out of all proportion to the difficulty of this process. In this way, our narratives are not simply reflections of reality but movements that create new meaning. Much of my writing starts with conversation. What a rare gift it is to find a person as passionate and intrigued by the same themes that intrigue oneself. Some find such a conversationist among their professional colleagues. I am so thankful that I have found this friend in my wife, Mary-Anne.

It is not the absence of influences that define new meaning and unique concepts but, rather, the unique combination and reconfiguration of existing concepts. As such, if there is anything fresh or unique in the ideas presented here, I am deeply indebted to the many influences and conversations I have had over the years with friends, students, and books. There is no way I can mention them all by name. Our online students at *mimesis.academy* engage us weekly with the most beautiful questions and insights.

There are, however, a few I can and must mention by name. They are the brave ones, who offered to review some of the earlier manuscripts. Thank you, Harry Haver and Tonya Stanfield for your patience and encouragement. In my desire to connect the big ideas and clarify the big picture, I often failed to see the detail - such as the finer points of grammar! Thankfully, grammar is a big deal to some of our friends. So I want to especially thank Kathryn Hannula, who has read and reread the manuscript numerous times and offered many helpful nuances. If any errors remain, it's because of my stubbornness to ignore her suggestions. But more than her keen eye for detail, it is her passion for this message that has been an inspiration throughout.

ABBREVIATIONS

Different translations of the Bible are used throughout and indicated with the usual abbreviations. The following two are new and therefore get special mention here:

DBH   The New Testament: A Translation by David Bentley Hart

RA   The Hebrew Bible: A Translation by Robert Alter

REVIEWS

In reading *Creative Chaos* by Andre Rabe, I discovered to my joy that theology can still be both intellectually profound and profoundly moving. Rarely in recent years have I come across such an excitingly transformative reflection on the hidden meaning of Christianity. Informed not only by biblical scholarship but also by the sciences and an awareness of the brutal history of human violence, this succinct work digs deep beneath conventional Christian thought in search of enlivening currents of meaning crusted over by centuries of dubious religious assumptions. Readers will find in this surprising text that both Christian teachers and their sophisticated opponents have too often blunted rather than exposing the meaning of divine creation, redemption, the crucifixion, and resurrection of Jesus. I strongly recommend this book as one not only to be read but also reread.

- **John Haught**, Distinguished Research Professor in the Department of Theology at Georgetown University.

Andre Rabe's latest work is his essential re-imagining of the Christian meta-story. With easy, deft hand and keen theological instincts, he guides us through Scripture, Genesis in particular. Understanding the first book of the Bible as a back-and-forth of the unconscious and conscious selves, he demonstrates how the God of creation is seeking continually to tease human beings forward, to the depth of relationship which is love. The anthropology of René Girard forms a leitmotif, revealing how humanity began on the wrong footing of violence and rivalry, and yet in Christ a new-and-true way of being human is offered, one of nonviolence and forgiveness. Christ thus "re-sets the trajectory of the human story." The outcome is a holistic, healing narrative of seduction to love, so different from the divided, unhappy legacy of the old reading, with its damaging binaries of paradise/fall, heaven/earth, perfection/sin, grace/law. Rabe's work represents an epochal moment of fresh reading, one that is happening in many ways throughout Christianity but is given here what could very well be its classic presentation. This book overcomes violence not simply in the obvious, physical sense, but as the very key to existence which has framed everything for human beings, including the interpretation of the Christian message itself. According to Rabe, it is exactly all this which God in Christ is saving us from.

- **Anthony Bartlett** Ph.D. Theologian and author, including *Seven Stories*

Andre says, "You cannot be certain and astonished at the same time." In *Creative Chaos*, he expertly walks through the origin stories, archetypes, and symbolism gently challenging traditional certainties that may hold us back from new possibilities. Humanity has been unconsciously shaped by narratives. The ideas presented here push the narrative forward in thought-provoking ways, challenging us to ask entirely new questions. *Creative Chaos* invites us into a chaos that is not evil, but the deep waters over which the Spirit hovers and creates new life. Jesus is presented as a model of how to live in a posture of openness to a God that will continually surprise. It's a challenging, refreshing perspective which opens doors you may not even know were shut. I highly recommend this book to anyone who is up for a fresh take on what they've held as certain or who desires a new adventure in their spiritual journey.

- **Tonya Stanfield**, Masters in Christian Spiritual Formation and Discipleship. Author of *Traffick Proof - A Counter-Human Trafficking Tool.*

God is not a rival, vying for control of your life. Turns out, control is not the goal. This book is a summons to set out on the adventure of maturity; through myth, rabbinic midrash, patristic thought, psychological insight, Girardian anthropology and Biblical contemplation to new possibilities for life. Beyond the lack within, beyond a blueprint from above, beyond being a spectator on the sidelines, beyond chaos being met with coercion, the Spirit beckons you to a beauty unimagined in the depths we fear.

- **Jarrod McKenna**, award winning nonviolence educator and host of the popular InVerse Podcast.

Preface

Chaos may seem an unlikely source of creativity, but below its senseless surface lies a swirling depth of possibilities. Every person enters a world that is already filled with symbols, meanings, and stories. No one starts with a blank canvas. Rather, we find ourselves thrust into a matrix of narratives. Yet, something truly new is possible amid this chaos. Time is a space in which these stories can be reassembled, reinterpreted, and ordered in a way that gives particular meaning to my life.

Our stories can be more than a reflection of reality; they can transform experience, inspire new action, and in so doing, transform our reality. *"And the word became flesh."* That is how the Gospel of John describes the event in which divine ideas became tangibly real in the person of Jesus. Text, words, and ideas are not meant to remain intangible - they are searching for embodiment.

This book is a journey through thousands of years of symbols and narratives that point to the underlying reality of our existence. We follow the development of consciousness through the stories humans have told, beginning with myths that are older than the Scriptures. The biblical text marks a definite progression in human awareness, and within the context of the Bible itself ideas continue to develop.

The perspective given here might be new for many, but the aim is to provide more than simply an alternative interpretation of Scripture. Rather, I hope to show the connection between the inherent human capacity to create meaning, the depth of the text we have at our disposal, and the measureless gift of the Spirit of truth drawing us forward. An inexhaustible mystery lies enfolded in each of us. How it unfolds in your story is an unprecedented unique event. This living narrative reached a crescendo in Jesus. In him, we see the mystery unfolding in flesh and we receive an invitation to share in his consciousness.

Each of the chapters in this book is a progressive step in understanding and opening up human consciousness. Ultimately we want to receive the kind of unitive awareness Jesus spoke of when he prayed: "I have given to them the glory you have given me, *that they may be one just as we are one.*"

The mysteries of time, self, narrative, and meaning are all intertwined. And our part in the mystery is more than passive explorers - *we are invited to co-create.* In Chapter 1 the metaphor of music is used to explore the nature of reality and the role we have in shaping it. How we give value to our life events is not always obvious - much of it is hidden from our awareness. Events gain significance in the context of a story. Similarly, our individual stories gain meaning in the context of larger stories.

Understanding the processes by which we construct our stories and create structures of interpretation is of great benefit. Chapter 2 explores the fascinating relationship between the conscious and unconscious. That enigmatic part of us, which does not submit to the logic of time and order, can also be a rich source of new meaning. Jacob's ladder is a beautiful metaphor of the connection between the known and the unknown, the earthly and the transcendent. A healthy co-operation between the conscious and unconscious gives us the benefit of a story grounded in reality, yet open to astonishment.

As a child develops, so do the stories he or she tells. Humanity as a whole also developed through different stages of consciousness and this development can be traced in the way our stories evolved. The Genesis origin stories are for many the context in which they understand their own existence better. And indeed they are a rich source of meaning. An important discovery of 22,000 cuneiform clay tablets was made relatively recently. They contained myths similar, in many ways, to the biblical narratives. Chapter 3 looks at these pre-genesis texts to gain insight into the development of the human mind and what they reveal about the Genesis texts.

The mythic symbols of the unconscious provide a new depth of interpretation as we re-discover the wisdom of Genesis. Mythos is the unconscious subtext over which the Logos is written and creates a new context in which to re-read the Genesis origin stories. In Chapters 4 and 5 we begin the adventure of understanding anew the Yahwist origin texts of Genesis 2 and 3. We begin here because these stories are older than the Genesis 1 account. By reading them in this sequence we can better appreciate the development of the story. These narratives are not simply concerned with ancient history. They are the narratives of every person's development. It is your story; your becoming; your genesis.

Talking animals and magical trees are completely absent from the Priestly source - the author of Genesis 1. An obvious development in thought has occurred. The conscious and unconscious enter into a more mature relationship in these texts and the results are beautiful! Chapter 6 explores how the writer of Genesis 1 re-imagines the beginning and thus, the significance of the present.

These alternative readings bring into question many of the popular concepts taught from these first three chapters of Genesis. For instance, the concepts of "original perfection," "the fall," and "original sin." These are either invalidated or completely re-defined by this radical new reading. The concepts of the fall and original sin profoundly influence the way people understand themselves. Transforming these concepts therefore transforms the meaning of our own stories.

In Chapter 7 we work through these implications and discover that some of the most original interpretations of Genesis, those of Irenaeus of Lyons for example, are surprisingly relevant to what we have uncovered. The aim however is not to give comprehensive theological arguments but to introduce these alternatives. The appendix provides book recommendations for those who want to delve deeper into these themes.

Chapter 8 introduces another layer of interpretation through the work of René Girard. We again look at myths but from a new perspective. And, in the light of this perspective, we discover how Scripture subverts and converts the meaning of symbols and the message of myth. The pattern of these stories are not restricted to ancient myths - they are reflected and relevant to our own life stories.

When such fundamental concepts such as origin, fall, and creation are redefined, they have profound implications for how we understand the person and work of Jesus Christ. If salvation is not a restoration of some imagined original perfection, then what is it? If chaos is not an evil outside of us, but a source of inexhaustible meaning within us, how does Christ help us transform this inner relationship? And, if the God of possibility invites us to co-create, how does Christ demonstrate this in a way that is relevant to our lives? The last chapter is a celebration of Jesus Christ in transforming our reality into something much richer and more open to unfolding beauty.

CHAPTER ONE

Invited into Mystery

I will solve my riddle to the music of the harp.

- Psalm 49:4

Music is a language not yet confined by words. It communicates values that move us, yet cannot be defined. There is a mysterious appeal to these suggested meanings - a message is present and its beauty resonates in us, yet it remains a riddle. The sound registers and we are simultaneously aware of what we hear and unaware of its full interpretation. It vibrates in both the conscious and the unconscious, and we find such seductions to explore the enigmatic - the hidden meanings - irresistible. Music echoes in a part of us that is similarly unexplained, uninterpreted, unknown.

The self that I am conscious of - the self that is known, formed, interpreted, and well explained - began here, in the realm of the unformed. As these fragments of uninterpreted messages find meaning, a story is born; from the unformed chaos, self is born. Underlying this self-conscious story are the unconscious fragments and the processes of interpretation that we are only vaguely aware of.

MYSTERY FOUND A VOICE

My wife and I were once invited to a piano recital in a very unique location - a mansion that lay on the rugged edge of a coastal nature reserve. As we entered the home, my attention was first drawn to the collection of paintings artfully displayed throughout the house. A handful of guests were helping themselves to the delicacies, but something more intriguing was luring me. A spectacular vision of ocean, mountains, and sky, spilling through the large lounge doors was drawing me to the outside patio.

Like an elegant lady waiting for her date to arrive, a grand piano stood expectantly in the far corner as the sun was enjoying its last hour of wakefulness. Moments later her date arrived. The pianist took his seat and the conversations came to an end.

A new sound filled the air.

The gentle breeze seemed to join in with the melody and the waves rhythmically danced along. Rays of light skipping across the ocean became audible, every color a different note and every movement part of the harmony.

The music was unfolding what was present everywhere. Mystery found a voice. As each note flowed from the revelation of sounds that came before, the connection became so clear: The significance of the present note can never be isolated to a single sound. What moves me in the present sound is all that flowed before. The notes that came before somehow still resonate and impart to this present note its particular meaning. It inherits the beauty of what precedes it.

And yet, the present sound is more than the sum of what came before. It is both summary and source, conclusion and inception, an ending that anticipates a new beginning. It contains both the richness of its history and the promise of what might yet be. The present is pregnant - a testament to its intimate past and a glimpse of an embryonic future that exceeds the past and present combined.

Music envelops the mysteries of time, self, narrative, and meaning. The flow of time is manifest in the movement, the sequence, the change, and the rhythm of notes. As the melody develops, hints of meaning accumulate and a narrative begins to unfold. Experiencing this flow and the questions it evokes, would not be possible without consciousness. We can tease these themes apart and discuss each separately for the sake of simplicity, but in reality, they remain intertwined. There can be no self without time. Neither would there be any narrative without self. Nothing would be known of time without a self to perceive and narrate it.

MUSIC AND THE MYSTERY OF TIME

Rhythm, duration, tempo, transitions, beginnings, and endings are all part of music ... and time. Both evoke questions of meaning. Modern life is divided into hours and minutes. Value is often measured by how productive we can be within those hours. When is the next appointment, how long will it take, and will this meeting be a recurring event? When, how long, and frequency partly describe our experience of time. But time is much richer than that. Years, months, days, hours, and seconds are all measurements of movement. One cycle of our planet spinning around the sun is a year. A day is how long it takes for our earth to spin around its axis. The movement is real, but is that all there is to time - a measurement of movement? If we reverse the movement, would time be reversed?

Einstein showed us that time is indeed real but more mysterious than our measurements of cosmic movements. Time is also related to gravity and speed. You may wonder what this has to do with you. The gravity of your life story is very much intertwined with the reality of time. The connection will become clearer, but let's continue with Einstein's thoughts about time. He discovered that time is not one thing, but that time passes differently, for instance, in the mountains than in the valleys. A person living at a higher altitude ages quicker because time passes faster! If this person meets up with a friend who lives in the valley after a few years, the one who lives in the valley would have had less time to think, less time to live and would have aged slower. The relativity of time is no longer a theory. Various experiments, including those with atomic clocks, have proven it.[1]

You may wonder how can it be that the person on the mountain had more time than the person in the valley if they both spent five years in their respective locations. The answer is simple. Our measurement of five years is not an accurate measurement of time. It is a convenient measurement for it allows us to plan our meetings and schedules, but time itself is more complex. What difference does this make? Why is this significant to the meaning of my existence? After all, the difference that gravity and speed make to the duration of time is minuscule. What is important in this discovery, is not the difference in the duration of time, but the very nature of time. There are as many times as there are points of reality. *"Times are legion: a different one for every point in space. There is not one single time; there is a vast multitude of them."*[2] Time is made up of unique movements of relationship, not of a sequence of instances that are the same everywhere. It is therefore not this present moment that constitutes reality but rather this unique configuration of relationships. Consequently, there is no universal present, for there is no universal time. Your time is as unique as you are. Your present is your presence.

We may speak of music in general but it is the unique melodies that capture our hearts. In reality, music does not have a general existence but consists in the real events of songs and melodies. Similarly, time does not have a general absolute existence but is realized in the unique configuration of relationships. We have theorized about time in general for so long that we have come to believe it has an independent existence. That is like theorizing about music without hearing and moving to the melody. Time only becomes real in the life you live, consequently, your time is as unique as the relationships that form you. Narrative creates, preserves, and evokes the meaning of time.

MUSIC AND THE MYSTERY OF SELF

Time is personal. It can move slowly or quickly. Time also has an irreversible direction. Our kids grow up, we get older, and a glass falls and shatters, but we never got younger and a shattered glass never reassembles accidentally. Our experience of time includes a past, a present, and a future.

The present is not bound to an instance measured by a clock. If I am asked what I am presently doing, I might answer that today I am working in my garden. My awareness of the present is therefore situated as a day within this week. I could be aware of this moment within this day; of this day within this week; of this period of my life within its whole span between birth and death. My present, therefore, is as wide and as large as my awareness.

The significance of the present note can never be isolated to a single sound. Neither is the significance of this moment isolated. We locate ourselves not in seconds or instances but within the sequence of a story. Multiple narratives converge in my existence. Time becomes human in our narratives. These narratives include memories of the past and expectations for the future. We remember the past, but we remember it in the present. Similarly, we anticipate the future but we can only do so in the present. Awareness can include memories, present stimuli, and future expectations. In this way, the past is present.

But the past is present, not only in memory but also in the very fabric of reality. Wherever we are within this melody, the current note resonates with all the notes that came before. Every moment of existence pulsates into reality and transfers itself to the next impulse. I do not mean this only in an abstract poetic form. On a technical and scientific level, several billion quarks pulsate in and out of existence every second to form the elementary particles of every atom. At the smallest level of reality we do not find substances, but events. Although inaudible, the substance of reality is musical - vibrating, pulsating, rhythmic movements.

Is this strange? We more often describe our world as things, rather than events. Is the chair I sit on a substance or an accumulation of events? Am I a being or a becoming? Plato thought the world was made of substances and that relationships were attributes that did not change the essence of these substances. His ideas still influence much of the modern world's thinking. But for all the beauty and usefulness of his ideas, they also contained fundamental flaws. We have come to understand that relationships are not optional extras but the very movements that constitute reality. It is the process of becoming that is the very essence of my being. I cannot be without becoming. Verbs describe existence more accurately than nouns.

MUSIC AND THE MYSTERY OF MEANING

Occasionally, we ponder the brevity of our own existence in the context of cosmic time. Compared to the age of our universe, the times of our lives might seem insignificantly small. But it is in the fleeting appearance of human consciousness that the most significant questions of the meaning of time occur. As a flower blooms and passes away, there is a beauty of awareness invested in human consciousness out of all proportion to its earthly duration. The symphony of the universe only becomes audible in human questioning.

Let's return to the piano recital. The music was unfolding what was present everywhere. Mystery found a voice…

Not everyone in the audience experienced the unity and richness of the event. Some were distracted by the environment and hardly paid attention to the music. Others closed their eyes to give their exclusive attention to the music. And others still, were not there at all, preoccupied with other events, lost in their own minds. Each person's experience of reality will always be unique and subjective, but there are ways of enriching experience. We can each move from being a detached observer to being a co-creator of our reality.

On one level we might listen to the music and be entertained; on another we might see the beauty of the environment and be impressed; on yet another we might feel the breeze and the rays of light and for a moment remember that we are alive. But we have not heard the music until we've heard an invitation. We have not fully seen until what we see seduces us.

What makes such moments so enchanting is that they offer us an invitation, a call only heard in the deepest part of us, to participate in creating their meaning. There would be no crescendo, no harmony between the sound, color, and movement if I did not enter into this invitation and co-create its beauty.

Reality is in part constructed by consciousness. Yes, things may exist apart from our awareness, but they do not exist in the same way as they do when we become conscious of them. The music, the movements, the mountains, and the magical evening colors were uniquely brought together to exist in consciousness in a way that they did not exist in isolation. And the sublime beauty of these relationships would not exist without consciousness. Consciousness participates in creating beauty, meaning, and goodness.

THE SYMPHONY ANTICIPATES YOUR SOUND

A fully functional inner ear is formed by the time the fetus is four and a half months old, even before the brain is fully formed. The capacity to receive messages is integral to what makes us human. Even if the physical capacity to hear is impaired, a person will adapt to find another way of receiving messages. We can hear the melody of existence even before we know that we are part of it. The sounds are more than noise ... they are questions asking us for meaning; they are messages seeking interpretation; they are connections opening paths to communion.

Moving from the womb into this world brings about a new clarity of sound. The muffled noises become more distinct, yet what they mean, and what I mean in the midst of it all, can be overwhelming.

> Day to day pours forth speech,
>
> and night to night declares knowledge.
>
> There is no speech, nor are there words;
>
> their voice is not heard;
>
> yet their voice goes out through all the earth,
>
> and their words to the end of the world.
>
> - Psalm 19:2-4 RSV

The author expresses what people have always sensed: that the whole cosmos is telling a story of enormous significance. But why am I given the capacity to appreciate it? Why have I been given consciousness? What does this vast story have to do with my story?

The single musical note finds greater beauty in the sequence of a melody, and so the significance of your existence is amplified by being part of a larger story. In you, the past is summarized. All that came before still resonates and imparts to you a particular meaning. And yet, your existence is more than the sum of what came before. It is both summary and source, conclusion and inception, an ending that anticipates a new beginning. It contains both the richness of its history and the promise of what might yet be.

Our experiences cry out for interpretation. Every event wants to be part of something larger as every note desires to be part of the music - its significance is found within its context. And so, when an event is made part of a narrative it carries the gravity of a history and vibrates with the possibilities of a future. Yet all of this beauty does not reside exclusively in the event itself but in the meaning consciousness (you) gives it.

We give our personal stories value by placing them in the context of a larger story. Throughout human history, stories have been created to give form to what we intuitively sensed. We remember a beginning before our conscious existence and we anticipate a future larger than our physical existence. A remarkable similarity exists between these stories of origin across many diverse cultures that had no contact with one another.

Why do we tell these stories? And why do we tell them in the specific ways we do? Do these myths have any basis in reality or are they pure fantasy? How does our understanding of these larger stories influence our experience of the present? To unravel the riddle of our beginning is an adventure like none other.

It is here on the creative edge of chaos, where all the past moments are still resonating, seeking closure, and all the potentialities of the future are drawing and pulling this moment forward, that we have a uniquely creative role to play. Our capacity to interpret the past and envision the future make humans more than passive bystanders to reality, more than spectators to this symphony. We are entangled actors. You exist because you have been invited into this reality - you are welcome in this universe. The symphony anticipates your sound.

Endnotes

1   Taylor, Edwin F.; John Archibald Wheeler (1992). *Spacetime Physics: Introduction to Special Relativity* (2nd ed.). New York: W.H. Freeman. pp. 84–88. ISBN 978-0-7167-2327-1.

2   Rovelli, Carlo. *The Order of Time* (p. 16). Penguin Publishing Group. Kindle Edition.

CHAPTER TWO

Matrix of Meaning

Do you hear the invitation? Something truly new and beautiful is possible for you. You are more than a spectator to the inevitable rush of time: You have the freedom and capacity to shape reality and give it value. Your story is a unique part of this cosmic symphony.

Some stories travel a predictable path and end up exactly where they planned to go. The further they develop the more rigid they become, protecting and preserving the meaning of their narrative. By the end, they mean exactly what they intended to mean from the very start. This might seem like a good thing, but such stories are also the most boring. They slowly lose the ability to keep anyone's attention, and eventually, they are forgotten.

Other stories are filled with surprise. At times they seem to fall apart because of unexpected tragedies, and at other times joy is restored in ways that could never have been foreseen. Meaning is

transformed ... even the beginning gains new significance from
the perspective of the end. These stories are alive, engaging and
enticing. What is it that keeps us open to astonishment? How can our
life stories remain open to possibilities? And how can the meaning
of our existence continue to unfold?

CREATING MEANING

Grammar is the structure of language and necessary to make
language understandable and meaning possible. Grammar does
not specify the meaning or impose a design upon the stories that
may be told. Rather it creates an environment in which the creative
process of meaning-making can take place. Within the boundaries
of these rules, you are free to construct concepts and say what has
never been said before. The framework gives the possibility of
meaning, not meaning itself. *When I see God you can create meaning & all a new*

Could it be that God is not an entity creating and controlling
the narrative, one who is manipulating events and giving value
to everything but, rather, *God is the possibility of meaning*? What
an extravagant gift of freedom that would be! As grammar is the
environment that makes creative storytelling possible, so God is the
environment that makes all creativity possible. But just as grammar
does not tell any story, so God does not create anything without
inviting creatures to co-author their stories and so co-design and
co-create themselves. Jesus demonstrates what this creativity
looks like when God and a human find freedom in each other. This
Christological thought will be developed in Chapter 9.

If I have an active role in creating the value and beauty of my
life, it would be very useful to understand how this process works.
My life events constantly cry out for interpretation. And each of us

develops interpretive frameworks by which we give meaning to
these events. As mentioned earlier, these interpretive structures
can become rigid - echo chambers - where we only hear what
we already know. The richness of life's symphony is replaced by
a monotone voice. Every event confirms what we believe. We no
longer hear the invitation; we are no longer seduced by the other.
Is there a way of being both logical and imaginative; reasonable
and open to the transcendent?

   The more certain we become of who and what we are, the fewer
opportunities we'll have to be astonished. For possibility can never
be reduced to certainty. If something is possible it is not certain, and
if it is certain it is no longer a possibility. We cannot be astonished
and certain at the same time, for we do not experience astonishment
and certainty in the same way. In that moment of surprise we have
to choose: do I want certainty or truth? The beauty of truth is not
something we possess, but an invitation into an adventure of the
unknown. We are surprised exactly because something outside of
our frame of reference is challenging our stability. It is this moment
of doubt that opens us up to a faith much richer than what we've
known so far.

   Why I?

   - Genesis 25:22

   Rebekah is the first biblical character who questions her own
existence. Before this question, the story began with barrenness.
Despite the freedom we have to construct our own narratives, we
often reach a dead end. The meaning of our existence becomes
exhausted ... barren. Our stories grow old and stale. We become
overly protective of what we believe and certain of what to expect.
We settle for the security of the familiar and lose touch with the

source of creativity and the capacity to invent. The unintended consequence is that life becomes boringly predictable.

Rebekah is barren, but her husband, Isaac, prays for her and something wonderful happens - she conceives. Rebekah's pregnancy is a profound metaphor for discovering the other within the self. This is a shocking new experience for the stable, centered and self-sufficient person. There is a part of me that is known, and a part that is not as obvious; a part I am conscious of, and a part I am not. Fruitfulness, new life, and new possibilities begin with recognizing that there is more to me than what I have known so far. The framework within which I create meaning needs to expand to allow the other, the unfamiliar and the unknown, to grow.

One cannot conceive new meaning and remain the same shape. Rebekah's pregnancy opens up a whole new complexity as she experiences turmoil within herself. To move out of the comfort of my familiar self can be difficult. "*Why I?*" It is because of this newfound complexity of the other within the self, that she seeks God's counsel.

God, however, does not return her to a stable, centered, and simple state. Rather, God confirms her disunity!

Two nations—in your womb,

two peoples from your loins shall issue.

People over people shall prevail,

the elder, the younger's slave

- Genesis 25:23 RA

Dr. Avivah Gottlieb Zornberg, in her book *The Murmuring Deep*, comments on this text:

> *God's words to her communicate an elusive, ambiguous mirroring of her own disunity. In a sense, God is confirming her experience of fragmentation, separation. ("Two nations shall split off from your bowels …") Her children, her interiority, are to be both alien, separate, absent—from each other and from her—and eternally present to her. Her life is forever bound up with them, her "I-ness" constituted by the interplay of conscious and unconscious aspects of experience.[1]*

Much like Rebekah, each one of us is pregnant with otherness. There is more to me than the self I am certain of. Becoming aware of the complexity of conflicting voices may be uncomfortable, even unbearable, but it is exactly this discomfort that opens me up to greater understanding and fruitfulness.

Human consciousness is not only a perspective of the world around us but is also uniquely turned in on itself. I do not only contemplate what I observe, but I also reflect upon my own signifi-cance. For in this pursuit of meaning, something truly mysterious happens - the very process of meaning-making comes into focus and becomes aware of itself. The mirror folds onto itself and an infinite complexity unfolds. Twins are born. They share a likeness, yet they are not identical but rather inverse and opposite in many ways. Both the conscious and the unconscious contribute to the stories we tell. It is exactly this complexity, these multiple voices, this other within the self, that gives the narratives we construct such richness.

I realize that each reader might already have established ideas of what is meant by the conscious and the unconscious. These pre-existing concepts might be helpful, but they may also cloud what is communicated here. This is a vast subject and I hope not to bog you down with technicalities. Therefore, I have limited the scope of this chapter to how this relationship between the conscious and unconscious influences the way we tell our stories. Understanding the story-teller is essential for understanding the story. So I ask you to lay aside, for a moment, your pre-existing ideas of what these words mean and simply enjoy this text for what it says in its own right. Now let us explore the wonder of this meaning-making phenomenon - human consciousness.

NON-IDENTICAL TWINS

There are many developmental stages in human consciousness, but one of the most fundamental is the process by which the conscious self emerges from the unconscious. Babies enter this world without being self-conscious - a pre-conscious stage. But soon after, self-consciousness begins to develop. To read the stories of Esau and Jacob as metaphors for the unconscious and the conscious can be illuminating. During a conversation with one of our online students[2] (and friend), this reading was suggested. I've been surprised at how fruitful this interpretation has been as I applied it to these characters.

> And the first one came out ruddy, like a hairy mantle all over, and they called his name Esau. Then his brother came out, his hand grasping Esau's heel, and they called his name Jacob.
>
> - Genesis 25:25-26 RA

The stories of Jacob and Esau are inseparably intertwined, each adding value to the other. Esau is the firstborn, in the same way as the unconscious comes into existence before the conscious self. Even at birth, his ruddy and hairy complexion hint at his wild, unrestrained and unrefined nature.

Each one of us begins our existence in a pre-conscious state. The unconscious is the firstborn in this sense. But this does not mean that nothing intelligible is happening here. As mentioned earlier, the inner ear is formed even before the brain is completely formed. Messages are received, stimuli are perceived. Hints of meaning and unformed images abound, but no established framework of interpretation exists and so the unconscious remains wild. In this unrestrained space, messages take on a unique form. Without the constraints of sequential time or formal logic, the symbols formed here appear chaotic when viewed from the perspective of the conscious.

It is essential to understand that despite what seems to be untamed chaos, is also a state of wholeness and peace. Prior to the emergence of a separate self, all is one. A pre-conscious baby does not distinguish yet between itself and the reality around it. Everything that happens and all that exists is part of a whole. This pre-conscious state is a kind of paradise of blissful union. There is no separation here, no lack and no desire, no good or evil. Everything simply is. These pre-conscious memories are preserved even after the emergence of the self.

There is another very significant aspect of the unconscious. It is more than an individual psychological phenomenon - it is where the boundary between self and all else disappears; a point of contact with what lies beyond self. The unconscious enfolds a great depth. Some have glimpsed this depth and tried to better define it. Carl Jung spoke about the collective unconscious. This

intuitive knowledge is not personal. In other words, it was not
gained through the experience of an individual but, rather, is
collective and gained through the experience of the species.
Just as animals are born with instincts specific to their species,
so humans inherit a pearl of intuitive wisdom. Layers of experience have accumulated through many generations to form a
pattern of knowledge.

But the unconscious is deeper still. It enfolds a depth beyond
intuition, beyond even the collective human history. The Scriptures locate the unconscious as the space in which God often
meets with us in surprising ways. The Bible is filled with stories
about dreams - unconscious events - in which wisdom is given
and meaning unveiled. There is no neatly defined boundary
for the unconscious, and it might be this very lack of boundary
that allows the divine to merge with our humanity.

Esau is the firstborn and that implies a certain priority.
The unconscious, formed first and given the inheritance of a
collective wisdom, is a prior necessity for the conscious self
to come into being.

Grasping Esau's Heel

Jacob, the conscious, follows not far after, "*his hand grasping
Esau's heel.*" This gives us foresight and insight into the competi-
tive, even rivalrous, way in which this relationship will develop.

For the conscious-self to come into existence it must disrupt
the peaceful wholeness of the unconscious. Its birth is an
awakening; it is a fight against the sleepy unconscious; it is for
Jacob to dispute the priority of Esau. The early moments of

conscious awakening are quickly overcome by weariness. Babies love their sleep. The seduction of this restful bliss cannot be resisted. For the conscious to succumb to its lure is to lose control, to sleep, to disappear, to trust that 'I' will be brought into existence again by something else I do not know.

[handwritten: back into awareness / The awareness of the / reasons]

And so the emergence of the conscious is a conflict that disrupts the tranquility of paradise and greatly impacts what and who we are. This disruption transforms the unconscious. Intuitions and memories of union are now contrasted with experiences of sepa- ration. And so the unconscious continues to develop beyond its pre-conscious origin. The awakening of the conscious is a type of trauma. Neither the unconscious nor the newly formed conscious is fully prepared for this new phenomenon. The initial stages of this separation are filled with confusion and conflict. At different ages, this conflict takes on different forms.

AND THE LADS GREW UP

And the lads grew up ...

- Genesis 25:27 RA

The unconscious is not only operative when we sleep, and neither is the relationship between these two parts only rivalrous. There is also the mundane, day-to-day co-existence of the brothers Esau and Jacob as they grow up together. Both are part of one family, yet they experience, interpret and remember their life events dif- ferently. Isn't it amazing how members of the same family can be so different? Some psychologists describe the unconscious and the conscious as two systems.[3] The messages we receive through the experiences we have are inscribed twice - once on each of these systems. But these systems operate by fundamentally different rules and, consequently, the way each system interprets messages and generates meaning is not identical. This double inscription creates a matrix of meaning.

Have you ever focussed on solving a problem for an extended period of time with no solution in sight? But then, while not giving it any conscious attention and busying yourself with something completely different, the solution suddenly presents itself. A thought process obviously continued without your conscious awareness.

The following example demonstrates that memories are inscribed and recalled differently from the unconscious than from the conscious: This morning I was writing down some memories of when Mary-Anne and I first met. I recalled several events and how our relationship developed. Some of the details from decades ago have faded, but others were still clear. Suddenly I was swept into a different world. Something happened that was more than a calculated recollection - a memory was triggered on a completely different level and I was transported back into a moment that occurred more than 30 years ago. The whole event, the emotions, the feelings, and every detail were vividly experienced again as if no time had passed. This timeless dimension is a typical characteristic of the unconscious. Maybe 'timeless' is not the best description. It seemed as if no time passed and every relationship within that moment was recreated. The order of an irreversible time was suspended, for time does not work the same in the unconscious as in the conscious mind. Even if I tried to consciously preserve such an experience, I would not be able to recollect it with such clarity or immediacy. The event was inscribed and recalled from a different dimension than the conscious way in which we remember and the whole process happened involuntarily.

Let me give one more example to show that the unconscious can express itself physically: We live in the beautiful coastal town of Hermanus. One of our favorite habits is to swim in the marine tidal pool. One sunny day, when Mary-Anne and I began swimming our laps, I had trouble with the rhythm of my breathing. As usual, I took a breath, then took a couple of strokes and attempted to breathe out while my head was underwater before coming up for another breath. But for some reason, I could not breathe out underwater. Stopping, I made sure my sinuses were clear and tried again. No. I could not release my breath underwater and experienced a sense of anxiety. As I sat down on one of the rocks and contemplated what just happened, a memory flashed back from when I was a 5-year old. While growing up with two older brothers, there was a stage when they were allowed to swim in the big pool, but I was restricted to the baby splash pool because I did not know how to swim yet. One day, when my two brothers were off to school and my mom was distracted, I slipped out and headed for the big pool. I jumped in and quickly reached the bottom. This is where the memory began. I kicked the bottom to reach the top again and gasped for air. The next descent down was slower, for this time I did not have the momentum of jumping in. My toes barely reached the bottom and consequently I could not kick hard enough to reach the top again. The clarity of this memory was amazing. The pool stairs were not too far from me and I wondered how I could reach them. Thankfully, at that very moment, someone reached into the pool and pulled me out. A teenager living in the same housing complex saw me from his window and ran to help.

This event, which I had not thought of for decades, suddenly affected me physically. The unresolved fear of that moment was manifesting in my body. When submerged in the water I held onto every breath for dear life. As I realized what caused this, I sat back and spoke to myself: "You are not drowning. You know how to swim. Be at peace." I took a few deep breaths, swam to the bottom of the pool and sat down holding a big rock to keep me down. I turned my focus inward and just allowed the calm and peace to be my awareness. After half a minute I breathed out and remained underwater for another half a minute. Jacob and Esau were conversing and solving this problem together. *conscous f measen.*

If memory is compared to a painting, our conscious memories are painted over unconscious memories. If our lives are compared to stories, then our conscious story is written over the text of the unconscious. Or if we use again the analogy of music, remembering the illustration of the piano recital, then the unconscious can be likened to a different instrument. Let's add an upright bass to this analogy. It's an instrument that requires a different skill set to play, produces a unique sound, and has its own musical score. It is possible that the piano and bass play two different songs and in so doing they would frustrate each other and the beauty of neither is heard. But if they could harmonize, each giving the other space and opportunity, the result would be a much richer sound. Jacob's story is never complete by itself. There is always the background story of Esau, drifting in and out of focus. Esau seldom speaks up, but he is always around. This other dimension, this primal unformed language, this alternative interpretation, creates an environment in which meaning can be enriched. What we think, say, and how we act is never as simple as it might seem.

What we say is spoken over the unconscious narrative. Our words contain more meaning than what we intend. We are never completely in control of what we mean. What we experience has depth beyond our immediate conscious awareness. This does not mean that we are enslaved to a system over which we have no control. In itself, this reality is neither good nor evil. It has the potential to be destructive or beneficial. But recognizing the complexity of this internal relationship is essential in the development of a more beneficial and harmonious co-existence.

This understanding can greatly enrich the way we read and interpret Scripture as well. Below the text is another text. The narrative is multi-dimensional. It requires interpretation and conversation. When we fail to recognize the other less obvious voice, when we ignore what may be implied and impose a singular meaning onto the text, we suppress the very life and conversation that the text invites us into. And such suppression leads to disharmony and even animosity. Yes, there might be comfort in having a clear and simple message, but such comfort is soon exposed as shallow - a monotone noise. For in the process of imposing a singular meaning, we exhaust the text of its meaning. Certainty strangles possibility. The living conversation dies as the text becomes ever more monotonous and its meaning predictable.

BIRTHRIGHT AND PRIORITY

And the lads grew up, and Esau was a man skilled in hunting, a man of the field, and Jacob was a simple man, a dweller in tents. And Isaac loved Esau for the game that he brought him, but Rebekah loved Jacob. And Jacob prepared a stew and Esau came from the field, and he was famished. And Esau said to Jacob, "Let me gulp down some of this red red stuff, for I am famished." Therefore is his name called Edom. And Jacob said, "Sell now your birthright to me." And Esau said, "Look, I am at the point of death, so why do I need a birthright?" And Jacob said, "Swear

to me now," and he swore to him, and he sold his birthright to
Jacob. Then Jacob gave Esau bread and lentil stew, and he ate
and he drank and he rose and he went off, and Esau spurned
the birthright.

- Genesis 25:27-34 RA

As they grow up, it becomes clear that Jacob is the more refined, civilized and simple. He controls his environment and dwells in structures that he himself has erected. Esau, in contrast, remains naturally at home within the wild, amongst the animals. The skill of hunting is, to a large extent, the skill of being present and grounded in the immediate environment. The hunt involves danger; it is a life or death situation for both the hunted and the hunter. Situations of danger have a way of making us more present to the moment. The unconscious is this primal hunter, naturally at home within this immediate chaotic danger.

It also becomes evident that Jacob is the more calculated of the two. He is in search of identity and more keenly aware of the future and, consequently, of the birthright inheritance that belongs to Esau. Esau, on the other hand, is unrestrained, impulsive, and not so obsessed by questions of identity and the future.

Remember the context: we are exploring what it means to be human and the uniqueness of consciousness. Esau and Jacob represent two aspects of our consciousness. And within the story above, Jacob desires the birthright and Esau desires the food that was prepared - the immediate gratification of his hunger. Desire is a major and unique theme in the development of human consciousness. Both Jacob and Esau are driven by desire. They are not identical desires and often need to be negotiated. And so the conflict for priority intensifies. Jacob has ambitions that drive him to attain what belongs to Esau. For the conscious to come into its full potential, it needs to assert itself to the extent of suppressing the unconscious. There is a period in which the child is happy to live somewhere between the two worlds of the imaginative and the reasonable, between the intuitive and the calculated. But a stage comes when a clear priority is chosen. Jacob must have priority. This is a necessary and natural evolution, for if imagination is not tamed by reason it will become ever more delusional.

In Robert Kegan's book, *The Evolving Self*,[4] he identifies the pursuit of meaning as the driving force behind personal transformation. I agree, but I want to draw attention to what energizes this process. How could there be a pursuit of meaning if there is not first a desire for meaning? So desire can be identified as the most fundamental force at the center of what makes the development of human consciousness possible.

What is desire? The invitation of beauty? The attraction of value? The magnetism of meaning? The intrigue of what is other? The excitement of new possibilities? The promise of being, of fulfillment? But why are we intrigued by beauty, attracted to value … why do we desire?

All these words - invitation, attraction, magnetism, intrigue, promise - assume some form of distance. In the pre-conscious paradise of undifferentiated union, there can be no desire, for there is no distance where there is no distinction. It is the very space between myself and the other that makes the movement of desire possible. Desire both affirms the distance and bridges it. To desire is to affirm a difference between myself and what is not self. There is no 'I want' if there is no sense of 'I.' But neither can there be a sense of distinction without the space created by desire. To be clear, after the development of a distinct self, desire can be both conscious and unconscious.

Desire forms in the space between reality as it is, and reality as it could be. Humans are not satisfied with perceiving reality as it is. We desire meaning. And in the pursuit of meaning a very powerful capacity develops to understand reality, not as something static, but as a movement that comes from the past and flows into the future. Consciousness of time gives us access to the logic of cause and effect and forms the basis of story-telling. It enables us to learn from the past, to accumulate knowledge and to anticipate the future. It opens up our understanding to the possibilities of the future.

In the story of Jacob and Esau, it is Jacob that displays this awareness of the future more keenly. It is the conscious part of us that is more aware of the logic of cause and effect, calculating and reasoning, to make a desirable future more likely. It is the independent self that takes control of the story and constructs a framework of interpretation - a tent in which he feels secure. The unconscious also generates meaning but in a more loose and unstructured way. It is less likely to settle on a definitive meaning and more likely to repetitively and imaginatively suggest many possible meanings. Think of dreams as an example.

Narrative Creation of Self

I am formed in a sequence of events. A multitude of events converges in my existence. But far from being neutral in this sequence of events, I create the meaning of these events. I am not simply the product of the events that happen to me, I am the interpretation of these events. Narrative both creates and preserves the meaning of these events. How does one make sense of all these relationships?

This question opens up the inner story of my life events. With every new experience, the skill of constructing a narrative grows. Over time a fairly reliable pattern emerges, a structure by which all new experiences are measured. Lessons from past experiences inform our expectations. As expectations are met according to our predictions, the interpretive structure is affirmed and the story gains confidence. Jacob is constructing a dwelling for himself in the midst of the chaotic wilderness. His voice is growing more prominent. The multiple influences that produce the unified 'I' become overly reliant on the influence of Jacob - the calculated, reasonable and civilized voice. Esau is still around, but we aren't sure where he is or what he is up to.

Within much of psychology and philosophy, this narrative-self or autobiographical self is seen as the very process by which self is constructed. Or let me say it another way: to a large extent, it is the process of meaning-making that is self. From our earliest moments of consciousness, we search for meaning. We wonder how events are connected. What is the common denominator? What gives significance to our memories? In this place of uncertainty, it seems that order will bring security and the best way of ordering events is to make them part of a story. Soon we discover there is nothing more central to our memories than the self that remembers them. There is nothing more common to my experiences than the 'I' that experiences them. And so, in these early stages of self-formation, I find my self in my story. The self, constructed by narrative, naturally becomes protective of the story that birthed it and continues to sustain it. If you find your self in your story, you often find your security in being right about your story. The pursuit of certitude is an early and necessary part of self-development. In this process, we lose touch with our ground, with our Esau. The imaginative fades as structured reasoning become more important. Jacob clears a space and constructs his tent. Here, within the space he controls, he can live a simple life. The unconscious is undermined for the most part as the newly formed self insists on its priority.

Narrative Identity & Illusion

As Jacob continues to carve out his own identity, he deceives his father to acquire Esau's birthright blessing. With the help of Rebekah, he prepares the kind of meaty dish his father loves. He also dresses in Esau's clothes and puts the hairy skins of the animals they just slaughtered on his hands. This is an elaborate scheme of deception.

Deception is only a possibility when a sense of a separate self has sufficiently developed. There is a stage when young children give us the most honest and often comical answers. But soon after they learn a new skill. Only when one perceives separation between self and others, does deception become an option. One may walk into the kitchen, see the cookie jar on its side and half-empty, and the toddlers with crumbs all over themselves. But when one asks: "Did you eat the cookies?" They shake their heads in denial while hiding the half-eaten cookies behind their backs. Deception indicates a significant development in self-consciousness.

It is also during this development that questions about identity become more prominent. When Jacob takes the dish to his father, Isaac asks: *"Who are you, my son?" And Jacob said to his father, "I am Esau your firstborn"* (Genesis 27:18-19 RA).

It is the pursuit of meaning and identity that leads to the rise and dominance of the conscious self. Yet the stories we tell ourselves and others are not always as simple as they seem. The haunting question: "*Who are you, my son?*" is often answered deceitfully. The conscious insists on being in control of the narrative it constructs, even if it is not entirely truthful. In this insistence on its own priority, the conscious becomes more rigid in what is allowed to become part of its story. The messages and experiences that do not fit into its structure of interpretation are suppressed. Who are you, my son? Are you indeed who you profess to be? Are you as simple as the story you've been telling yourself and others? The unconscious questions the validity and certainty of our conscious narratives.

At this stage, the conflict between Jacob and Esau comes to a climax. Whatever friendly relationship existed before will now give way to open rivalry. It is not so much the exchange that took place, when Esau sold his birthright, as the deceptiveness by which Jacob now assumes Esau's identity that causes conflict. When I become overly confident in my self-knowledge, presuming to have a firm grasp on my identity to the extent that I deny the presence of this mysterious other, an unhealthy conflict begins to brew. The unconscious does not simply accept the loss of its identity. The desires, messages, and experiences it wants to express will find utterance even if no room is found for it in the conscious story.

The relationship between Jacob and Esau comes to a complete breakdown and Jacob flees to a distant land because of his fear of Esau. There comes a stage in the development of consciousness where the logical is chosen above the intuitive and calculated reasoning takes dominance over the imaginative in such a way that a real alienation takes place between the conscious and the unconscious. It's a time during which we lose touch with our core ... yet it is a necessary stage.

Every metaphor has its limits, so I won't try and work through every detail of the Jacob and Esau story. However, two more events are significant in unraveling this relationship.

RECONCILIATION

Initially, the conscious self has to establish itself and guard against being absorbed into the unconscious again. Consequently, the unconscious has to recede. Despite this early and necessary conflict, the relationship continues to develop. For a person to be whole, this internal relationship must be reconciled.

To reconnect with our essence, to once again find our grounding, can be a long journey and often only happens in the second half of life. We have to learn again how to appreciate the wisdom of the unconscious. The reasonable and the intuitive, the calculated and the imaginative, must find a way to creatively work together to construct a story that is more honest and at the same time more open to surprise.

Jacob constructed a narrative-identity saying: "I am Esau" and with this took the birthright and priority of Esau. Despite this deception, he is blessed by his father. Yet this confusion of identity continues to haunt him until it comes to a climax in Beth-el. The hidden other erupts in a dream in which heaven and earth are bridged. It is divine messengers who bring his fragmented interior into meaningful relation.

He awakes and exclaims: Surely God is in this place and I, I did not know.

- Genesis 28:16

It is exactly in this unknown other, this I, I did not know, that God is present. (Zohar translates it: God is in this I, I did not know.) This whole encounter happens within the dream, the unconscious, but spills over into consciousness.

The unconscious is not necessarily a place of deep, dark secrets. Rather, its deep chaos can be the infinite source of new meaning as we allow the spirit of God to hover over it and draw out the beauty that is possible for it. *There is no fear in love* (1 John 4:18). Fear deforms the unconscious signifiers into the worst conclusions. But in the presence of the God who is love, something new is possible. When love becomes the environment within which new meaning is created, God is found within this I, I did not know.

It is after this encounter that reconciliation between Jacob and Esau becomes possible. It is also significant that the night before Jacob is reconciled with Esau, he has an encounter with God in which his name is changed. No longer would he be known as Jacob the deceiver but as Israel - one who has wrestled with God and prevailed. For me to move out of the realm of self-deception, I have to embrace this other part of me, this chaotic depth, this unordered, uninterpreted abyss. At first, Jacob is filled with fear at the very thought of meeting Esau again, but when they finally meet *"Esau ran to meet him and embraced him and fell upon his neck and kissed him, and they wept"* (Genesis 33:4).

There is beauty and truth in both the conscious and unconscious. The one is not a false self and the other a true self. Both are essential in the conversation that makes us who we are. When one is given undue preference we become less than what we could be. Ultimately the intuitions of the unconscious can be more weighty by appropriating the logic of the conscious, and the conscious self can experience the wholeness and wonder of the unconscious without having to abandon its rationality. Within this conversational matrix, the creation of meaning is much richer.

As we embark on an exploration of the Genesis texts and the many underlying narratives that contributed to these texts, I pray that we would once again discover the inherent wisdom of the unconscious. The hope is that both the logic of the conscious and the enigmatic symbols of the unconscious would become visible in these texts. Recognizing these dimensions will enable us to form new meaning and create new beauty.

Endnotes

1   Zornberg, Avivah Gottlieb. *The Murmuring Deep* (pp. 222-223). Knopf Doubleday Publishing Group. Kindle Edition.

2   https://www.mimesis.academy

3   including Freud, Lacan, Laplanche. For an introduction to the double inscription view see: https://www.lacanonline.com/2017/04/ whats-so-unconscious-about-the-unconscious/

4   Kegan, Robert. *The Evolving Self: Problem and Process in Human Development*. Cambridge, Mass.: Harvard University Press, 1982.

CHAPTER THREE

The Wisdom of the Unconscious

When stories first began they were alive and filled with wonder - not written on paper or stone but performed around tribal campfires where men and women inscribed them on the hearts of their children. These tales were not obsessed with facts, for the beauty and truth they desired to communicate had to be remembered. And it was only the most fantastic, the most captivating stories, that survived to the next generation. When, eventually, the skill of the written text was invented and these narratives were transcribed, much of what made them alive was lost. Yet, these texts preserved something of the wonder that was present in the original play.

These early forms of story-telling reoccur in the development of every child. The first pictures my children drew might not have been the best examples of refined art, but they carried a profound depth of meaning. The simple lines that represented a brother and sister holding hands spoke of a relationship of trust that no amount of artistic education could portray more honestly. At this stage of child development, the unconscious is less restrained. Impressions and feelings flowed without much filtering. I did not try to correct the perspective or discipline them for not using the correct technique. How inappropriate that would have been! No, I simply enjoyed the beauty of the truth they tried to portray. Similarly, God allows his kids to draw their pictures without needing to correct them at every opportunity. We have much to learn from the symbols of the unconscious. A wealth of wisdom and meaning lies hidden here.

Humanity in their infancy drew similar pictures and told fantastic stories. Today we refer to this genre of narrative as myth. Myth might well be likened to a different musical instrument, played according to its own rules, its own musical score. If we could only recognize this unique sound, we might again hear a much richer symphony. In these early stages of human development, the imaginary is more prominent than the reasonable; the untamed voice of Esau takes priority. This was a time in which humans were not as certain as they are today about what things meant, and consequently, many imaginative interpretations could be offered. The sun was more than a ball of chemical explosions, it was the blazing garment of God. The clouds were more than vapors of waters, they were heavenly chariots. Some of these poetic images were preserved in Scripture as well and they are as captivating today as when they first appeared (See Psalm 104). Yes, these creative interpretations may not be scientifically accurate, but they preserve an honesty and depth of meaning we can still benefit from.

Many find great value and meaning in the Genesis origin texts. But where and how were these stories birthed? If we could find the subtext, an insight into the dramas that played out around campfires long before these ideas were written down, that would add a whole new dimension to our understanding. What magical gardens and fantastic creatures flowed from the tongues of our ancient ancestors before they found their way onto papyrus scrolls? These are the unconscious texts over which the Scriptures were written. If we can trace their development, then we'll come closer to once again experiencing the astounding wisdom of the unconscious.

The sequence of the chapters in this book will follow the sequence in which these stories developed, starting with the most ancient myths that have similar symbolism to the Genesis texts, and then moving onto Genesis 2 and 3 - also known as the Yahwist creation accounts. It has long been recognized that the Bible consists of many documents written by many authors over an extended period of time.[1] The creation account beginning in Genesis 2:4 pre-dates Genesis 1. The later addition of Genesis 1-2:4, which most scholars see as a revision done by what is known as the Priestly Source, dramatically reframes the story.[2]

THE SYMBOLISM OF ORIGINAL UNION

The earliest stories humans told, from various cultures that had no physical contact with one another, contain remarkably similar symbols. Why would diverse and independent groups use similar symbolism to communicate their ideas? Was it similar events that gave rise to similar stories as the anthropologist and literary critic René Girard suggests or was it similar states of consciousness that produced similar symbols as some psychologists would argue?[3]

We'll first consider the psychological perspective that distinct states of consciousness produce specific symbols. The development of every child mirrors the evolution of the human race. In the same way every human develops from a pre-conscious 'baby' into a self-conscious person, humanity as a whole also evolved through different stages of consciousness. Each one of these stages produces symbols that portray the new realities assimilated by that stage of consciousness. We'll also consider the Girardian perspective in later chapters as we build multiple layers of meaning.

In the Indian Upanishads text, the egg symbolizes the process by which non-being becomes being. In parts of Africa the Calabash, a woody shell, is used to imagine the original container of all. The Chinese Wu Chi is the empty circle. It symbolizes everything before the beginning, prior to process and all other symbols; before time, before sequence, before anything finite. It is the eternal present and perfect infinity. The T'ai Chi is another circular symbol, but it contains all contradictions in one, light and dark, male and female, etc.,

The circle is an image of the undivided consciousness, before a sense of self is formed. There is no difference between the top and the bottom, between the left or the right of a circle. It also has no beginning nor end, and so represents a complete whole that encompasses all. The circular symbol developed into associated symbols such as the womb, the enclosed garden, and the circular serpent. These images of origin capture a form of paradise in which the divine is at rest.

Prior to the development of the conscious, all is one. The ego still lies dormant in this original bliss. The sequence of time and the logic of cause and effect play no role in this infinite and timeless realm. Here there is no contradiction, no separation, no conflict, no hierarchy, and no value system. The lion and the lamb lie side by side in peace. The beginning and the end meet; the alpha and omega are one.

BACKGROUND STORIES OF GENESIS

In 1849, in the ancient city of Nineveh, which is on the outskirts of the town of Mosul in modern-day Iraq, a most significant discovery was made. The palace of Sennacherib with its 71 rooms was unearthed. But something even more meaningful was uncovered … a library of 22,000 cuneiform clay tablets. Initial translations of some of the fragments revealed that they contained stories of creation, of gods enjoying their garden paradise, of a prototype human in search of immortality and a snake that stole it from him.

More than a hundred and sixty years later, scholars are still discussing how these stories are connected to the biblical accounts and how they can enrich our understanding of Genesis. What is clear is that similar themes, characters, events, and story structures to the Hebrew accounts were present in other myths throughout the ancient Near East. Canaan, Syria, Mesopotamia and to some degree, Egypt, shared a similar culture.[4] Smaller tribes and groups within this larger culture developed unique versions of these common stories but the connection between them remains obvious.

All the stories we'll examine here are older than the biblical accounts. How these myths evolved into their later and more complex forms is fascinating and many themes are relevant to the theological ideas present in the Hebrew Scriptures. It is also significant that many of these myths relate to the first 11 chapters of Genesis. What follows are short summaries of a selection of these myths, touching specifically on the themes they have in common with the Hebrew origin stories.

ENKI & NINHURSAG

Early Sumerian myths tell of the transformation of a wasteland into an ordered agricultural society with irrigation and gardens. Desert surrounded much of the fertile land between the Tigres and Euphrates rivers.

The myth of Enki and Ninhursag is a fascinating story of how the world came to be the way it was for these ancient Sumerians. The names of the gods and their offspring are obvious personifications of the elements and phenomena they observed in their world. Enki, also known as Ea in later myths, is the personification of wisdom and freshwater, both of which were essential for human survival.

There are a number of features in the myth that you'll find familiar when comparing it to the later Yahwist creation story. The following are the most obvious correlations:

- The setting for the unfolding of creation is a garden paradise.
- In it are plants that should not be eaten. Eating them results in the curse of death, yet the curse is withdrawn and death does not come immediately.
- Enki, the personification of wisdom, is implicated in partaking of the forbidden, yet he is also essential for the creative process.
- One of the female gods, Ninti, is "The Lady of the Rib," and is known as the one who gives life.

THE WISDOM OF THE UNCONSCIOUS

Dilmun is the name of this garden sanctuary and is described in the opening poem as follows:

> Pure is the city -
> and you are the ones
> to whom it is allotted!
> Pure is Dilmun land!
>
> …
>
> When all alone
> he had lain down in Dilmun,
> the spot where Enki
> had lain down with his spouse,
> that spot was virginal,
> that spot was pristine!
>
> …
>
> In Dilmun the raven
> was not yet cawing,
> the flushed partridge
> not cackling.
> The lion slew not,
> the wolf was not
> carrying off lambs,
> the dog had not been taught
> to make kids curl up,
> the colt had not learned
> that grain was to be eaten.[5]

Paradise is often imagined as a historical state of existence before the entrance of death or any other imperfection. However, the original ideas around this garden paradise were not so much a pre-death state of perfection, as they were a description of pre-creation. It is not that the wolf was once vegetarian and thus lived peacefully with the lambs but, rather, Dilmun is a place before either the wolf or the lambs came into their natural existence. As such we can recognize this space as the pre-distinction state of the pre-conscious.

It is in the garden paradise called Dilmun that Enki and Ninhursag fall in love and produce their first daughter. He also produces offspring with the consecutive daughters.

Enki and Ninhursag produce Ninsar - Lady of Vegetation.

Enki and Ninsar produce Ninkurra - Goddess of Mountain Pastures.

Enki and Ninkurra produce Uttu, The Weaver of Patterns and Life Desires.

After impregnating Uttu, he leaves Dilmun to continue his work. Uttu, however, is upset and tells Ninhursag what happened. Ninhursag instructs Uttu to take Enki's seed from her body and plant it in Dilmun. She does this and eight plants grow as a result. When Enki returns and sees the plants, he starts eating from the first one. It is so delicious that he eats all eight of the plants. Ninhursag finds out about it and she is mad and curses Enki to death. Consequently, Enki becomes sick and begins to die. None of the gods can help him and no one knows where to find Ninhursag. However, a fox knows where she is and brings her back to Enki. She begins a healing process by which she asks Enki where the pain is, then draws it out of him into herself, and then gives birth to a god. Eight gods who are beneficial to mankind are born this way:

- Abu, god of plants and growth;
- Nintulla, Lord of Magan, governing copper & precious metal;
- Ninsitu; goddess of healing and consort of Ninazu;
- Ninkasi, goddess of beer;
- Nanshe, goddess of social justice and divination;
- Azimua, goddess of healing and wife of Ningishida of the underworld;
- Emshag, Lord of Dilmun and fertility;
- and Ninti, "The Lady of the Rib," who gives life.

When reading the myth of Enki and Ninhursag, it reminds me of a dream. Images are scattered and the usual laws of logic and morality are not as prominent. There are hints of meaning, but they are not clearly defined. Much room is left for creative interpretation. Maybe the myth is partly an interpretation of a dream. What is obvious is that meaning is suggested by scattered symbols, which is more consistent with the way the unconscious communicates, than the conscious.

ENKI AND NINMAH

The myth of Enki and Ninmah explores some very popular creation themes, namely gods seeking rest, rebellion, and the reason for creating humans. There was a time when the senior gods made junior gods work too much. They complained bitterly and a solution was sought. Enki and Ninmah began a competition to see who could make suitable replacement laborers (humans). Various prototype humans were formed, but they were all rather pathetic and suffered from many disabilities. Finally Enki produced what looked like the most pathetic candidate of all - an infant. Yet it proved to be the best design for it could grow, mature and pass away naturally.

This is a profound intuition - the idea that a creature could participate in its own creation. The process by which a helpless infant transforms into a capable human has benefits. Wisdom is gained through the journey.

As we'll see later when we consider the Girardian perspective, there might be real historic events behind the stories of rebellion and the need for faithful laborers. Yet, the pursuit of meaning amid these circumstances is again more consistent with the suggested meanings of a dream, than a conscious retelling of historic events.

ATRAHASIS

The myth of Atrahasis develops the same themes in a new era. The problem of laborers is addressed again, but it also adds an explanation for natural disasters like the flood.

The junior gods, who were subject to forced labor, caused an uproar. Their noise deprived the senior gods of rest, specifically Enlil who is Enki's (Ea) father.

Ea proposes a solution, namely to slay the leader of the rebellion and use his blood, mixed with clay, to form a new prototype laborer. Seven pairs of humans are created, but a vital mistake is made. Ea forgets to make them mortal. (These semi-gods are the literary forerunners to the Nephilim in the Hebrew Bible.) Another mistake comes to light - the rebellious blood with which they were created continues to stir rebellion in the humans. They too begin to disturb the rest of the gods.

The only solution, it seems, is to reduce these rebellious and noisy humans with disasters. When Enlil plans to annihilate the human race with a flood, Ea warns Atrahasis (one of the seven pairs of experimental humans) of the plan and instructs him to build a boxlike boat. Atrahasis does as Ea instructed and loads two of every animal into the ark. As a result Atrahasis and a selection of animals survive the flood. His first act after setting foot on land again is to offer sacrifice. This might be seen as a way in which Atrahasis accepts his proper place of servitude to the gods. Enlil loves the smell of the sacrifice and agrees not to annihilate all life if a proper limit to human life could be set. And so an agreement is reached in which Enlil promises not to annihilate life again and Atrahasis accepts that humans should be mortal and serve the gods.

What is the proper relationship between humans and the divine? This is a significant question for the Atrahasis myth, and it is bound up with the question of human mortality. The story makes the imaginative leap to suggest that there once were humans who were immortal, but that such an arrangement did not work. Conflict and disasters only increased. Part of its message is that humans should make peace with their mortality

Adapa

Besides the similarity of the names Adapa and Adam, many other aspects of the stories are connected. Adapa also means "human" or "earthling." Similar to Adam he is also the first created human. When Ea created Adapa, "*He granted him wisdom, but he did not grant him eternal life.*" This is the central theme of the myth. Humans are intelligent enough to contemplate the meaning of time and the inevitability of death. But in knowing we will die, what then is the point of life? Would immortality not be an appropriate gift? Like Adam, Adapa has an opportunity to eat the food of immortality, but because he listens to Ea's warning he is robbed of the opportunity.

One day, while Adapa was out fishing, a wind capsized his boat. In anger, Adapa curses the south wind and breaks its wing so that it could not blow for seven days. But this act seems to be overstepping the proper human boundaries and Anu, the sky god, sends for Adapa to come and explain himself.

Ea advises Adapa to show remorse and humility. Ea knows that Anu might offer Adapa the food and drink of life. But Ea advises Adapa not to eat or drink anything he is offered as it would surely be the food and drink of death. When Adapa appears before Anu, he does exactly as Ea instructed. Anu, impressed by Adapa's intelligence and attitude, offers him the food of immortality, but Adapa refuses.

> "Why has Ea revealed to impure mankind
> The heart of heaven and earth? A heart
> ... has created within him, has made him a name?
> What can we do with him? Food of life
> Bring him, that he may eat." Food of life
> They brought him, but he ate not. Water of life
> They brought him, but he drank not. [6]

Anu is surprised by this refusal and asks why he does not partake. Adapa tells Anu of Ea's instruction. The third tablet is fragmentary, but it seems Ea would be punished for this act. And so Adapa returns to earth to live out the remainder of his days.

IMMORTALITY & WISDOM

A few underlying questions are present in all these origin myths, namely the reality of death and the human capacity to anticipate this event. They recognize that humans have been gifted with a unique intelligence. However, this gift of wisdom also presents us with unique problems: we are wise enough to know that we will die. Why would the gods share the gift of wisdom with humans but not the gift of immortality? What is the purpose of life in the face of inevitable death?

Consciousness is in itself an experience of freedom - an awareness that I am more than a physical entity, determined by events beyond my control, and swept along the inevitable flow of time. I can act; I can create; I can give meaning to events. It is not a freedom from the physical but rather a freedom within my bodily existence. But this feeling of transcendence is confronted by the reality of death. Death is a limit to our freedom and questions the meaning we create. Death consciousness focuses our attention on the significance of time. If humans were immortal, it's unlikely that we would have pursued the meaning of time with much urgency.

Why are we mortal? Two solutions are explored in these pre-genesis myths. The first is that the original humans were created immortal, but that became a real problem to the gods, as they became very noisy or rebellious. The imagined solution was, therefore, to kill them off unnaturally through disasters until a final agreement was reached to limit human life to 120 years. The second explanation proposes that humans were created mortal but given the opportunity to become immortal. This opportunity however was forfeited.

In both cases, the stories simply give an explanation for what was plainly obvious: humans are mortal despite our intelligence. Somehow we need to make peace with this reality. Whether these stories helped their ancient audience any more than it helps us, I'm not sure. What we do know is that we still face the same reality of death, which stirs questions of meaning.

The Yahwist author used many of these familiar themes, settings, and events to skillfully craft a story that gave a new vision of both God and humanity. But in order to see what is new in the Yahwist account, we first need to recognize what is a continuation of the previous traditions. We'll explore these in greater depth in the chapters to come, but the following preliminary observations are useful now. The intelligence of ha-adam is on display in the naming of the animals. And, the personification of wisdom in the form of the serpent has obvious correlations with other myths of this time. The possibility of immortality that seems so close, yet remains out of reach, is portrayed in the tree of life. And death-consciousness also enters the story in Genesis chapter 3.

The Yahwist seems to give a unique perspective on this familiar problem. Humans are indeed created mortal - from the dust - yet, there is also the possibility of partaking of the tree of life. Immortality is therefore not an inherent quality of being human, but it may be received as pure gift. The Yahwist's God does not seem to have a problem with sharing the tree of life with humans. In the story, however, humanity also forfeits this opportunity. But is that the end of the story? It may be the perfect setup for a surprising twist.

The Garden and Creation as a Process

The concept of creation out of nothing was not familiar to any of these authors. Rather, creation begins in the midst of chaos. Some form of primordial material is always assumed. The time before creation is described as a time before civilization, before irrigation, when the land was a wasteland. The later popular Christian idea of creation-out-of-nothing meant that the garden paradise stories were interpreted as post-creation dramas and that makes it difficult to understand their intended meaning. Originally these stories described the very process of moving from pre-creation into the created reality that we now observe.

Consequently, in these mythic origin accounts, creation is also a process, not an instantaneous act. Specifically the creation of mankind seems to always be an experiment that progresses slowly. At the early stages of creation, humans are described as more animal-like, having no clothes and drinking water like beasts. The creation of humans is seen as a work in progress, an evolution. This ancient intuition has proven to be closer to the truth than later theories of instant creation.

The process also implies that the gods can be rather naive. Their works are not perfect and they often make mistakes, regret what they have done, and sometimes try to annihilate their mistakes. We might find it rather comical that the gods were naive in their experiments, but it provided a realistic perspective on an existence that was obviously less than perfect.

Let's give our attention specifically to the Yahwist account again:

This is the history of the heavens and the earth when they were created, in the day that the Lord God made the earth and the heavens, before any plant of the field was in the earth and before any herb of the field had grown. For the Lord God had not caused it to rain on the earth, and there was no man to till the ground; but a mist went up from the earth and watered the whole face of the ground.

- Genesis 2:4-6 RSV

The concept of creation out of nothing is absent here also. Similar to contemporary myths, creation is the act of bringing order to an existing chaos, of transforming a wasteland into a garden. The situation before this creative process is described as a time before culture, before plants grew or people tilled the land. The creative events of watering, of planting a garden, and of people tilling the land bring order to the chaos. The Sumerian myth of Enki and Ninhursag also mentions a subterranean watering system.

Throughout Genesis 2 we see a similar progression in the creation of ha-adam, the earthling. After creating the earthling Yahweh realizes that ha-adam is alone and that this situation is not good. He promptly creates animals in the hope that it will relieve the loneliness. However, no suitable partner is found among the animals. And so it's back to the drawing board, in a rather literal way. The earthling is placed in a deep sleep and the woman is separated from the male. At last a solution is found!

But the process is not complete. Further development takes place as the earthlings progress from their naive innocence into wiser, yet more conflicted, adults - people we recognize to be like ourselves. To interpret such a progressive creation as the work of a naive god, is one way to see it, but a greater wisdom might lie hidden in this approach.

Contrary to what is often assumed, the garden paradise was not created as the perfect, deathless abode for humanity. An actual historic state of deathless perfection was never imagined to be the meaning of this mystic garden in these narratives. Rather, it was a divine resting place prior to creation itself. The absence of death, of lions slaying their prey and wolfs carrying off lambs, was due to the fact that there were no lions nor lambs to begin with. The very creation of distinction and consequently of death-awareness would take place as the story ran its course. The mythic garden of Dilmun, for instance, was originally purposed for the enjoyment of the gods, not for the enjoyment of humans. Similarly, Eden is planted by Yahweh and humans are only placed in it afterward.

Rest is another important theme. Both the garden and the temple symbolized this space for rest and enjoyment. The temple was not so much a place of worship as it was a space for the deity to rest in. However, the deities' rest was often disturbed for two reasons. One, a garden needs labor and two, the laborers complained about all the work. The clear purpose for human creation in these early myths is to provide labor. Again, the garden was not created for humans, but rather humans were created for the sake of the garden! This was probably well understood by an ancient audience as it was made explicit in many of the myths. The Yahwist account contains traces of the same idea, stating in verse 5 that there was no man to till the land. Yet it soon becomes obvious that humanity plays a more significant role in the Yahwist account than in many of its contemporary myths. With that in mind, let's consider the unique trees that were present here.

The Lord God planted a garden eastward in Eden, and there
He put the man whom He had formed. And out of the ground the
Lord God made every tree grow that is pleasant to the sight and
good for food. The tree of life was also in the midst of the garden,
and the tree of the knowledge of good and evil.

- Genesis 2:8-9 RSV

Yahweh planted a garden. What we learned from the preceding myths is that the garden was not primarily intended for the humans but for the enjoyment of the god/s, in this case, Yahweh. Could it be that the two trees - the tree of life and the tree of the knowledge of good and evil - should be understood as first and foremost existing for the enjoyment of Yahweh? Be that as it may, the author does imagine Yahweh to be extravagant in generosity, for in verse 16 humans are invited to eat freely from any tree, except one.

The same kind of landscapes are described in the myths and in Genesis 2:10-14 - a fertile land between rivers. But the land needs to be worked. It is therefore significant that Yahweh has to take Adam and place him within the garden. It could indicate a movement from hunter-gatherer communities into agricultural communities.

The place of humans within this garden takes on a whole new form and meaning. We were invited into this space, and our creation continues here. The creative process comes to fulfillment when the earthlings enter a world that we recognize as our own. That is a world of complexity in which labor, pain, and death are part of the beauty and richness of our reality.

DIFFERENCES BETWEEN MYTH AND YAHWIST ACCOUNT

No Theogony or Divine Violence.

Most of the myths contain elaborate stories of where the gods come from, of how they are related, and of various conflicts between them. In contrast, YHWH *simply is* for the Yawist author. This Creator needs no explanation for he is as evident as creation itself.

It would seem to me that the Yahwist's understanding of God developed and consequently changed what could and could not be said about God. There is an implicit move toward monotheism, which is not simply a matter of arithmetic - one instead of many - but a whole new category of understanding. I do not presume that the move to monotheism was complete in Genesis 2 and 3, but rather that it was in process. The many varied speculations and divine dramas, so prevalent in the older myths, no longer had a place within this new understanding of what God is.

The kind of violent conflicts always present within these early divine dramas, are completely absent from the Yahwist account. In fact, the first act of violence would be ascribed to human jealousy. This is a most significant development, for violence is not glorified and justified by appealing to its divine nature. Rather it is condemned. Does this show an awareness of the way we have projected our own violence onto the divine? Whether it was a conscious realization or not, a radically new vision of God is presented, one in which God is not in competition or rivalry with anyone.

Focus on Humanity - the known.

Moving away from the pure speculation of the earlier divine dramas, also gave new impetus to focus on the subjects that humans can say something about - themselves. And so the nuances of human development, the exploration of human desire, temptation, and pursuit of wisdom receive greater attention than in most of the previous myths. Volumes of books have been written, inspired by the Yahwist's insights into the human condition. In this too, there is a definite development in consciousness between the pre-biblical myths and Genesis.

With these stories and suggested meanings hovering in the background, like the vague memory of a dream or the tonal background painting on a canvas, let us now re-read the Genesis origin stories and see what new meaning we may create.

Endnotes

1   Friedman, Richard Elliott. 1987. *Who Wrote the Bible?* New York: Summit Books.

2   Batto, Bernard F. 2014. *In the Beginning: Essays on Creation Motifs in the Bible and the Ancient Near East.* Winona Lake: Eisenbrauns, pg 46

3   See, for instance, Neumann, Erich. 2015. *The Origins and History of Consciousness.*

4   For an informative resource of ancient myths see: https://www.ancient.eu

5   Jacobsen. n.d. *The Harps that Once....: Sumerian Poetry in Translation.* Yale University Press. pg 185

6   Robert W. Rogers from his 1912 work, *Cuneiform Parallels to the Old Testament*

CHAPTER FOUR

Divine Seduction

On a recent walk on the beach, we came upon a delightful scene - the innocent joy of toddlers running around naked. There were screams of ecstasy and uncontrolled laughter as they bumped into one another. At this stage of human development, the individual ego has not fully formed yet and without a self to be conscious of, there are no filters to experience, no hindrance between desire and its fulfillment. Unashamed and without personal borders, they continued in this naked bliss as several adults paused to witness this scene with a sense of *déjà vu*.

On one level, there was a distant memory of my own childhood paradise. I recognized this naive innocence, this shameless nakedness, this borderless, self-less joy. But the more immediate memory was of our children at this age. I wished I could experience my two-year-old kids again. Parents often express such nostalgic longing, saying that they wished their children could have stayed that age forever. How short our memories are! Few parents who currently have toddlers are likely to make the same wish.

PRE-CONSCIOUS MEMORY

There seems to be a universal memory of an original perfection, a peaceful paradise, a whole that includes all, a timeless union. In many different cultures this intuition is symbolized with some form of circle. It is the original whole from which all things are born.

When we try to describe these memories, it is the conscious mind attempting to communicate these pre-conscious impressions. But these experiences are not easily communicated with the constructs of the logical mind. Images and symbols are more suited to envelop the meanings and impressions of this stage of consciousness. Symbols encompass huge areas of meaning precisely because they do not have a definitive meaning. The infinite space of the unconscious needs a language not constrained by words. Symbols are inherently more open to interpretation. And so, the circle and the enclosed garden came to be universal symbols for this timeless, infinite wholeness from which we originate. It is relevant to both the emergence of consciousness in individuals and the emergence of consciousness in human evolution.

The persistence of these intuitions of an original wholeness is due to two things. Firstly, the memory of union is based on the real experience of the pre-conscious state of every human. Secondly, this individual experience, in many ways, follows the same pattern of the development of consciousness in the human race as a whole. The pre-conscious state of humanity's infancy is experienced again in the development of every child. So both the collective unconscious, and the personal experience of the pre-conscious child both affirm this memory of an undivided paradise.

What I hope to demonstrate later is that this awareness of union is not the naive misunderstanding of an undeveloped mind but an authentic participation in reality. Although the conscious mind will bring a recognition of the separation between entities, there remains an underlying unity. Christ is nothing less than the one in whom all things consist, according to the author of Colossians (1:17). And in union with him, we may once again partake of this wholeness, experiencing our completeness in him (2:10).

INTRODUCTION TO THE YAHWIST CREATION STORY

The stories in Genesis 2 and 3 are very much an exploration of human development, of the emergence of consciousness, and the complexities that make us human. As such these stories are the stories of every human being. It is your story. But there is also another level of meaning - the development of human consciousness as an archetypal memory. An archetype is a way of representing all in one, and so Adam and Eve become the personified representatives of every man and woman.

We'll explore these Genesis narratives with this perspective - witnessing the unfolding of human consciousness. Compared to the myths we looked at before, we'll witness a definite progression in the narrative. The text is much more aware of the movements and processes that make us human. It has also removed some of the more fantastic heavenly adventures and elaborated the more grounded, earthly processes.

If today we begin reading a story where the main characters are a man called *Human* and woman called *Life*, we would immediately recognize what type of literature we are busy with. Adam is not a proper name, but simply means the earthling. Most of the instances referring to Adam also include the definitive article - *the* - which is not used with proper names. The text speaks of *the* earthling (ha-adam). This again shows that we are dealing with an archetypal memory which is part of the collective unconscious.

We will follow the story of the earthling as he becomes more recognizable as one of us. For of what relevance is ha-adam, created in the likeness and image of God, if we cannot identify with this earthling? The earthling begins with no parents and no history. The complexity of relationship has not yet become part of ha-adam's reality in this initial state. There is no passion, no desire, no psychological movement … only a naive innocence. But as the story develops, new complexities are introduced and we begin to recognize ourselves in the story.

These stories illuminate the processes and qualities that make us human. They weren't meant to become legends of a once perfect world which we lost because the first humans ate from the wrong tree. In fact, some Midrashic commentators provocatively suggest that it is precisely the human that emerges after the event of partaking of the tree of the knowledge of good and evil, that is like God (3:22). One of the first Christian theologians, Irenaeus, also believed that this is primarily a story of human development and that God always intended for us to partake of the tree of the knowledge of good and evil so that we would be able to make mature value judgments. But in our haste we grasped for this gift pre-maturely.

BREATH OF LIFE

[T]hen the LORD God fashioned the human, humus from the soil, and blew into his nostrils the breath of life, and the human became a living creature.

- Genesis 2:7 RA

Some commentators want to draw attention to the intimate process of creation by comparing the formation of man to a potter molding clay. There is indeed an image of intimacy present in this account, but it has more to do with breath than with the image of a potter and clay. The problem is that dust is not clay. It does not have the same properties and cannot be formed the way clay can be. So what is the significance of the earthling being formed from dust?

It has been argued convincingly that dust refers to human mortality as can be seen in Genesis 3:19.[1]

It's also significant to know that puns are a regular feature in the Torah, and the word dust (adamah) is a pun for the word human (adam).

From the very outset of the story it deals with the themes of mortality and the nature of human relationship with God. The earthling is created mortal, finite, earthy, yet God breathes into his nostrils the breath of life which transcends the purely mortal aspect of human existence. The finite creature is given the capacity to participate in the infinite being of God. Yes, there is part of us that is earthy and temporal, but there is also a part of us that comes from beyond ourselves and opens us up to the transcendent - the breath of God. This capacity to transcend our limits, to be part of creation yet capable of transforming it, and reaching beyond its appearance to its underlying source and meaning, is unique to our humanity.

Paul Ricoeur describes this complexity as follows:

> Dwelling in my finite capacity is something infinite, which I would call foundational. Schelling speaks of a Grund, a ground or foundation, which is at the same time an Abgrund, an abyss, therefore a groundless ground. Here the idea of a disproportion arises which is suffered and not simply acted upon, a disproportion between what I would call the excess of the foundation, the Grund/Abgrund, the groundless ground, and my finite capacity of reception, appropriation, and adaptation.... Now rightly or wrongly, I take the problematic of capacity and excess, and therefore disproportion to be constitutive of human being.[2]

A week after writing the section on the *Breath of Life* above, I was present as my dad breathed his last breath. The frailty and temporality of human life were deeply impressed on me at this time. However, it was not the futility of time that impacted me but the opposite. It is exactly the temporality of life that makes it so precious. If anything is available in limitless abundance, it somehow loses its value. There is a way in which limitation increases value. We only have so much time to say what we want to say, to do what we want to do, to love as we desire to love, to be and become ... it is exactly the finite space we have in which to live that gives every moment value.

In many early philosophies, these human complexities developed into a dualism that split the human into distinct and opposite parts. In Gnosticism, the earthly part is seen as evil and despised and the spiritual part is seen as good and can be liberated through knowledge. No such hard dualistic border is drawn in the biblical text. God is the Author of both the earthy aspect of the human and the divine breath. The earthling is a union, albeit with paradoxical qualities.

And the Lord God planted a garden in Eden, in the east; and there he put the man whom he had formed (2:8 RSV).

God plants a garden - an ordered space in the midst of the untamed wilderness. This terrestrial world consists of both an unordered wilderness and an ordered garden. A parallel can be drawn to human consciousness which consists of both an unordered unconscious and the ordered conscious.

Wherever the earthling was formed, it was not in Eden, for God has to put the earthling in Eden after he forms ha-adam. God prepares a space and seduces man into functioning within this space.

How does God put the earthling in Eden? In verse 15 the same thought is repeated: "The Lord God took the man and put him in the garden." Rashi (a medieval rabbi and Talmud commentator) argues that God moves man with words, not force. It is through the persuasive seduction of words that the earthling leaves the chaotic wilderness and comes into the ordered garden. And so Rashi translates this thought as, *"God captivated/seduced man to enter the garden."*

Here, however, the word pitahu, 'He seduced him,' is disturb-ing. This midrashic translation makes seduction the first human experience— seduction by God. [3]

Anthropologically, this movement into the garden can be seen as the shift from hunter-gatherer communities to agricultural communities. God's involvement in human development is not one of control or force, but rather one of persuasion. God creates by letting be. God extends absolute freedom to his creation to evolve in whatever direction it pleases, yet he does draw us, influence us, even seduce us into the direction of greater community, greater consciousness, greater love. The themes of seduction and desire are central to these narratives. Desire is both a uniquely human characteristic and central to the way in which God deals with the human.

> And out of the ground the Lord God made to grow every tree that is pleasant to the sight and good for food, the tree of life also in the midst of the garden, and the tree of the knowledge of good and evil (2:9 RSV).

Again, the theme of desire is implied as the trees are described as pleasant to the sight and good for food. And two central symbols are introduced: the tree of life and the tree of the knowledge of good and evil. The themes of wisdom and immortality, so prevalent in most of the creation myths of this time, are introduced. Given the importance of these trees, much is lacking in their description initially. Were both trees in the midst of the garden? Maybe, but only the tree of life is so specified. Ambiguity and misunderstanding will also become important themes as the story develops.

KNOWLEDGE AND DEATH CONSCIOUSNESS

> The Lord God took the man and put him in the garden of Eden to till it and keep it. And the Lord God commanded the man, saying, "You may freely eat of every tree of the garden; but of the tree of the knowledge of good and evil you shall not eat, for in the day that you eat of it you shall die." (2:15-17 RSV.)

Richard Friedman, in his very helpful, *Commentary on the Torah*, says the following:

> Not good and "evil," as this is usually understood and trans-
> lated. "Evil" suggests that this is strictly moral knowledge. But
> the Hebrew word has a much wider range of meaning than that.
> This may mean knowledge of what is morally good and bad, or
> it may mean qualities of good and bad in all realms: morality,
> aesthetics, utility, pleasure and pain, and so on.[4]

Again the example of young children is useful. Prior to the development of an independent self, the child is immersed in their reality in such a way that no separation exists between themselves and their world. Consequently, there are no value judgments. Things just are the way they are. To make judgments about good and bad, an independent will, a judge, is necessary. Although such independence might be desirable, the development of self-consciousness will also introduce the consciousness of death. If there is no self to preserve, there is no death to fear.

We have often interpreted the pronouncement "*for in the day that you eat of it you shall die*" as a warning of punishment, but it could equally be read as a prophetic statement of the inevitable: Self-consciousness will open the door to death-consciousness. It is partaking of the tree of the knowledge of good and bad, this development in consciousness, that inevitably results in an awareness of death.

From an anthropological point of view, somewhere in the development of human consciousness, the awareness of death entered in a more obsessive way. Together with the consciousness of self, comes consciousness of time. And as we saw in Chapter 2, awareness of time gives us access to the logic of cause and effect and forms the basis of story-telling. It enables us to learn from the past, to accumulate knowledge and to anticipate the future. It opens up our understanding to the possibilities of the future... and one possibility in particular, death. Animals become aware of danger and will flee the scene or fight the danger, but there is no lingering fear of death that overshadows their existence.

Now why would God prohibit us from gaining such knowledge - the ability to make value judgments? Especially seeing that God himself partakes of this knowledge (3:22). Could it be that this prohibition is similar to the kind of prohibition we give to our young children? We don't allow our toddlers to play with knives because they don't have the capacity to do so safely. However, once they mature, we teach them how to handle dangerous objects and situations in the proper way. So this prohibition, to not partake of the tree of the knowledge of good and bad, might only have been relevant for a specific period.

Alone? Let's Make Some Animals!

Then the Lord God said, "It is not good that the man should be alone; I will make him a helper fit for him." So out of the ground the Lord God formed every beast of the field and every bird of the air, and brought them to the man to see what he would call them; and whatever the man called every living creature, that was its name. The man gave names to all cattle, and to the birds of the air, and to every beast of the field; but for the man there was not found a helper fit for him (2:18-20 RSV).

Something about the mythic stories of experimental human creations still resonates in this text. After creating the earthling, Yahweh discovers something about this situation that's not good.

And in the light of this, beasts are created - *"but for the man there was not found a helper fit for him."*

While writing this portion of the book, I'm taking some time out from my usual schedule to give my exclusive focus to this subject. I've come to stay on a friend's remote farm on the border of South Africa and Lesotho, an area rich in the ancient rock art of the San nomadic tribes that crossed this terrain thousands of years ago. The expansive mountains and valleys together with the endless blue sky give one a sense of space rarely felt within populated communities. The nearest small town is more than an hour away and only accessible by an off-road vehicle. The nights are dead quiet - not even a breeze.

My mind wanders to the small San tribes that traversed this area. They could travel for extensive periods of time without encountering another tribe. My few days here are giving me a small taste of the kind of loneliness they must have experienced. I am staying in a farmhouse apart from my friends and this morning they had to leave for a couple of days to collect necessary equipment. If I am not writing or reading, animals are my only companions. At least these are mainly friendly animals and good conversationists I might add, or more accurately, good listeners.

Imagine what the awakening of human consciousness was like in this vast landscape: the slow realization that despite the deep connection we enjoy with animals, something very different is happening in us. The tearing away of the conscious self from the world of unconscious unity brought our uniqueness and loneliness into stark focus. Traumatic is surely not too strong a word to describe such a disturbing realization. Language and symbols are ways in which we give expression to this excess of meaning - ways of letting go of the trauma. Our animal companions do not communicate on that level. The realization of separateness from our animal friends intensified the loneliness.

Is this the archetypal memory that is captured in the image of the earthling naming the animals? The very act of naming is an act of separation. If the earthling said: "You are called Lion," it is precisely because the lion is separate and different from the other named animals. And this act of separation, of naming, intensifies the loneliness. The first experiences children have of being alone, can dramatically shape the way they connect with others for the rest of their lives. This state of being alone is described as "*not good.*" God determines to make "*a helper comparable to Adam.*" The phrase "helper comparable to" is a very interesting construct in Hebrew. It speaks of a helper contrary or against - a mirror reflection, equal but opposite.

A COMPANION THAT OPPOSES

It is in this context of finding reflective relationship that God invites the earthling to name the animals. This is an invitation to co-create; for in the process of naming, ha-adam discovers the power of his consciousness to give meaning to his world. Something else becomes obvious as well. Every animal has an equal but opposite partner. It is both likeness and otherness that make intimacy possible. Maybe this quest that God calls ha-adam to, of naming the animals, is also meant to stir the question: What kind am I? What species am I to reflect? Ultimately this might lead to the depth of discovery of whose image and likeness humanity is meant to reflect. Is this another subtle seduction?

Such a contrary or reflective helper is first sought amongst the animals, but none is found. Remember, ha-adam is in the process of becoming human and we are following the drama of that development.

> So the Lord God caused a deep sleep to fall upon the man, and while he slept took one of his ribs and closed up its place with flesh; and the rib which the Lord God had taken from the man he made into a woman and brought her to the man (2:21-22 RSV).

In reading this story we often assume that Adam is male. But, as noted before, ha-adam simply means the earthling or the-one-from-the-earth. Many commentators agree that at this point in the story the earthling is both male and female. In the context of the birth of consciousness, sexual differentiation is irrelevant when there is only one. There are in fact two words that denote gender, Ish and Isha, but they will only be introduced after the earthling is separated in two. Consequently, some translations, and specifically the Zohar commentary moves away from the idea of a rib, and supports the idea of a side. The image being painted is of the earthling, being both male and female in one body, separated by God into two equal but opposing sides. Ha-adam now becomes Ish and Isha, a mirror reflection, a relationship in which a person can come to know himself or herself in another.

Does a deeper connection require a greater separation? Instead of an undifferentiated oneness, a new kind of intimacy requires union with distinction. Ish and Isha, this new distinction, opens a way for you to see yourself reflected in an image that is both opposite from you, yet like you. This is not sameness, but likeness. There is a depth and complexity of relationship that opens up in this helper that opposes me, and it is the very opposition, the contrary reflection, that helps to develop the self-knowledge that makes us human. Zornberg comments:

> God seduces him, God lures him to acknowledge his longing for a helpmate, God overwhelms him with sleep to collaborate with desire. According to one powerful midrash, Adam dreams the woman and wakes, pulsing with agitation, to the fulfillment of his dream. His mate emerges from an unconscious state, from a slippage of mastery.[5]

Just as God brought the animals to Adam, he now brings the woman. But in contrast to his effortless naming of the animals, he now seems to be unable to name her. Instead of the sober control with which he previously spoke, he finds himself in a dreamlike state in the presence of this other who confounds his language. It is no longer the power of his intellect or his control over language that is on display, but an experience that draws him beyond himself and causes his language to become poetic. If we relate this to the development of language in children, we see a remarkable similarity. The first words are those with which to identify or name others: "mama, dada, dog, ball." But it is when the child first attempts to describe a relationship and the emotions present in relationship that we find the most comical sayings. The complexity of relationship confounds language... but also draws it into a higher plane.

"This one, this one time, is bone of my bones and flesh of my flesh."

And as if he is unable to name her now, he speaks about a future event in which she shall be named. She would in fact only be named later, after partaking of the knowledge of good and evil. Maybe this delay in giving a personal name is also indicative that the process of forming a fully individual person has not been completed yet. These are the first recorded words of Adam. They reveal something truly unique about human consciousness - the ability to recognize ourselves in another. Being human cannot happen in isolation, rather it is the unique experience of *being-in-love* that constitutes the being of mankind.

Remember, it all began with an invitation to co-create. Ha-adam began creating meaning through the naming of the animals. But that is not where the co-creative process stopped. It is in relationship that the creative process is amplified. The reflective movement will continue to shape both Ish and Isha. It is significant that at this stage no announcement is made by God that the project has been completed, that the aloneness of man has been overcome and the goal of having an earthling in his image and likeness has been achieved. For that to happen we have to wait a bit longer.

and they shall become one flesh. And they were both naked, the man and his wife, and were not ashamed (2:24-25 RSV).

Consciousness becomes more complex as desire intensifies and diversifies. Yet the statement that they were both naked and were not ashamed also implies a childlike unself-consciousness. At this point in the story human consciousness has not yet developed to the place where we recognize it as our own, for it is not yet fully self-conscious. They are indifferent to their differences and consequently nothing interesting happens.

I suggest that the aloneness of humanity has not yet been overcome, precisely because they are so unconsciously one that there are no relational movements. There are no borders between Ish and Isha, for there are no fully formed individual selves. This situation is reminiscent of the toddlers playing on the beach. An unashamed oneness means they are still alone. The full scope of desire, including the intensity of both love and hate, has not been experienced yet. This naive innocence also has no trace of the complexities of both a developed conscious and unconscious. But these are the themes that will be developed in our next chapter.

Endnotes

1   Walton, John, *The Lost World of Adam and Eve*, See Proposition 8.

2   Ricoeur, Paul & Williams, James. (2011). *"Religion and Symbolic Violence."* Contagion: Journal of Violence, Mimesis, and Culture. 6. 10.1353/ctn.1999.0003.

3   Zornberg, Avivah Gottlieb (2009-03-30). *The Murmuring Deep: Reflections on the Biblical Unconscious* (p. 6). Knopf Doubleday Publishing Group. Kindle Edition.

4   Friedman, Richard Elliott. *Commentary on the Torah* (Kindle Locations 6631-6634). HarperOne. Kindle Edition.

5   Zornberg, Avivah Gottlieb. *The Murmuring Deep: Reflections on the Biblical Unconscious* (p. 10). Knopf Doubleday Publishing Group. Kindle Edition.

CHAPTER FIVE

Becoming Human

Serpent Symbolism

Genesis 3 begins by introducing us to the serpent: "*Now the serpent was more cunning than any beast of the field which the Lord God had made.*"

Modern Christianity almost exclusively sees serpent symbolism as evil. Consequently the serpent of Genesis 3 is identified as Satan without much further thought. However, the authors of this text had no concept remotely similar to our later developed concept of Satan. Many positive meanings were associated with the serpent at this time.[1] Jesus himself admonished that we should be wise as serpents. It is so easy to take later concepts and impose them on earlier texts and in so doing completely miss the intended meaning. It is of much greater benefit to first understand, as far as possible, the most ancient and authentic meaning and then allow that to inform our understanding of how these concepts developed.

I am not suggesting that the serpent symbolism is good instead of evil, but rather that it is varied, capable of symbolizing both good and evil, and as such it is a well-suited companion to the tree of the knowledge of good and evil. The Genesis text introduces this character as a beast made by God and wiser than all other creatures. If it was to be understood as the symbol of evil only, this would not be the way to introduce this creature. Both God and the serpent will present questions to the earthlings that will draw the conversation forward and eventually produce a man and a woman whom we recognize as being like ourselves.

Serpent symbolism was widely used during this time and in the area where the Hebrew stories were birthed. In typical Jewish style, the text uses a symbol that is well known but simultaneously subverts much of its meaning. I want to specifically highlight the meaning of the serpent symbol as it relates to consciousness. We observed earlier that prior to the emergence of the conscious, the independent self, the child is one with its reality. This original wholeness was often symbolized with the circle which has no beginning and no end, no above or below, only undifferentiated oneness. A widely used variation of the circle symbol is the circular serpent. The circular serpent symbol is also a further development in consciousness in that it includes distinctions not present in the circle alone.

Although absolute rest is something static and eternal, unchanging and therefore without history, it is at the same time the place of origin and the germ cell of creativity. Living the cycle of its own life, it is the circular snake, the primal dragon of the beginning that bites its own tail, the self-begetting 'Ουϱόβοϱος.'²

The Egyptian Ouroboros is a serpent swallowing its tail. The cycle of time, as evidenced by the rising and setting sun, the repetitive seasons and the flooding of the Nile, enveloped all of reality. The serpent consumes itself but also impregnates itself and gives birth to itself, containing within itself the mysteries of the cycles of time and all the processes of life and death. The Ouroboros preserves the memory of origin wholeness and timeless union. As such it is an image of the undivided consciousness before the self is formed. It is relevant to both the emergence of consciousness in individual children and the emergence of consciousness in human evolution.

The earliest known occurrence of the symbol is on a golden shrine in the tomb of Tutankhamen, dated to the 13th Century BC. The name Ouroboros is actually Greek and means tail-devourer. The symbol made its way from Egypt into Greek mythology. A third-century Greek document has the Ouroboros encircling the words: "All is One." This image has been found all across the world - in Africa, Mexico, India and the Americas to name but a few. Not only do these symbols appear in ancient myths, but they persisted throughout time and similar intuitions still manifest in the dreams of modern humanity. Why?

THE AWAKENING OF DESIRE

The circular serpent preserves the pre-conscious memory of eternal union that includes all in one. At this stage consciousness is undivided. The self is still asleep in the perfect circle of unconscious development. What awakens it out of its slumber? What causes the eternal circular serpent, in which the whole is enveloped in

unconscious bliss, to lose its grip on its tail and break the circle?
What event provokes it to speak?

Maybe it is the prohibition, the confrontation with limitation:
"*you shall not eat.*" We know that prohibition somehow intensifies
desire. And it is the full awakening of desire that brings about a
duality in consciousness, a split, a conflicting voice. In this case
it is not the voice of the unconscious but rather the awakening of
the conscious that, for the first time, begins to separate itself from
the amoral unconscious.

Part of the emergence of the conscious self is a dissatisfaction
with simply accepting everything the way it is - a resistance against
being part of everything. Dissatisfaction and desire energize each
other. In separating itself from the unconscious and insisting on
its own independent existence, it also insists on separating itself
from the reality around it and making judgments about the relative
value of what it objectively observes, whether it is good or bad.
Remember it was Jacob who constructed his own dwelling and who
became occupied with questions of identity and inheritance. The
conscious self desires to know good and bad, instead of the bland
sameness of undifferentiated unity. Or simply, it desires good and
bad - to experience good and bad.

During this process of separation, a kind of confusion is inevitable.
What is still part of me and what is not? What is still within and what
is outside? "*the world of the dawn man is very largely an interior
world experienced outside himself, a condition in which inside and
outside are not discriminated from one another.*"[3]

This gives birth to a special kind of projection where internal
experiences are projected onto outer reality. This might be why
early man experiences the world as magical. An internal conversa-

tion can be projected in such a way that trees and animals become endowed with magical qualities. We have all observed children projecting their internal conversations onto external objects to make the drama more understandable.

WISDOM AND VULNERABILITY

Genesis 2 ended with these words:

> [T]hey were both naked (arôm), the man and his wife, and were not ashamed.

Chapter 3 begins with:

> Now the serpent was more cunning (arÛm) than any beast of the field which the Lord God had made.

The invention of chapters and verses came much later and so the connection for ancient readers, between arôm and arÛm, would have been even more obvious. A more common noun to describe wisdom would have been hkm. But the author artfully draws our attention to the connection between nakedness and wisdom by using the less common word arÛm. In other instances, arôm is used to describe vulnerability. Wisdom too requires a certain vulnerability, an openness to new ideas and suggestions. Wisdom is the ability to make sound judgments, and to do that there has to be a differentiation between good and bad.

As long as all is one, as long as the conscious mind has not divided itself from the unconscious, there can be no vulnerability. Vulnerability requires a border, an in and out, a self and not-self Vulnerability communicates two ideas at once. Without it one cannot truly be intimate, for it is this openness, this nakedness, that allows another to cross one's borders of isolation and penetrate the self. Yet this openness to intimacy also opens us up to pain.

Similarly, openness to learning is necessary to gain wisdom, but such receptiveness to new ideas can also produce confusion... even deception, with unintended consequences. This is an unavoidable conundrum: to gain wisdom one has to open oneself up and in so doing risk deception, and to be intimate one must become vulnerable and remove all protective borders. This might be the reason for the prohibition that Yahweh gave. Children need trusted guides, parents, to lead them into maturity where they may gain wisdom without deception. To pursue mature experiences before one is able to bear it, is indeed dangerous. It is not that Yahweh wanted to keep humanity in perpetual infancy, rather we were meant to mature with his guidance.

The serpent, being more wise and vulnerable than all the other creatures, can be seen as the projected voice of the emerging conscious self. It is this openness, which is essential to our humanity, that also creates the opportunity for temptation. Paul Ricoeur, in his brilliant book, *The Symbolism of Evil*, gives insight into the symbol of the serpent:

> In the figure of the serpent, the Yahwist may have been drama-tizing an important aspect of the experience of temptation—the experience of quasi-externality. Temptation would be a sort of seduction from without; it would develop into compliance with the apparition which lays siege to the "heart"; and, finally, to sin would be to yield.... The serpent, then, represents this passive aspect of temptation, hovering on the border of the outer and the inner; the Decalogue calls it "covetousness"[4] (Tenth Commandment).

THE KNOWLEDGE OF GOOD AND EVIL

*Now the serpent was more crafty than any other wild animal
that the Lord God had made. He said to the woman, "Did God
say, 'You shall not eat from any tree in the garden?'" The woman
said to the serpent, "We may eat of the fruit of the trees in the
garden; but God said, 'You shall not eat of the fruit of the tree that
is in the middle of the garden, nor shall you touch it, or you shall
die.'" But the serpent said to the woman, "You will not die; for God
knows that when you eat of it your eyes will be opened, and you
will be like God, knowing good and evil." So when the woman saw
that the tree was good for food, and that it was a delight to the
eyes, and that the tree was to be desired to make one wise, she
took of its fruit and ate; and she also gave some to her husband,
who was with her, and he ate. Then the eyes of both were opened,
and they knew that they were naked; and they sewed fig leaves
together and made loincloths for themselves.*

- Genesis 3:1-7 NRSV

At this stage no reference is made to Eve, but the more generic
term, the woman, is used. This helps to show the universal relevance
of the drama instead of isolating it to an actual person or one specific
event. She too is an archetype. The fact that the conversation
happens between the serpent and the woman further emphasizes
the more complete separation between male and female that is in
process. Individual selves are emerging.

Desire and questions are inseparably connected. It is the unknown,
the possibility of what might yet be, that stirs desire. Similarly, desire
multiplies questions and awakens the imagination to untold possibilities. An internal conversation about that which is prohibited is

projected onto objects that make the visualization process easier. Consciousness is no longer one undifferentiated perfection. This serpent no longer swallows its tail - it speaks. The all-is-one reality is unraveling. The conscious and unconscious are becoming more distinct. Male and female can now converse independently. And the blissful ignorance is now subjected to questions: "Did God say, 'You shall not eat from any tree in the garden?'" The conversation that follows is one we can all vaguely recall. For each of us has stood in this position where, for the first time, we argued against the prohibition; where we decided to grasp for what we were told was off-limits.

After the woman clarifies that there is only one tree they should not eat from, the serpent answers: *"You will not die; for God knows that when you eat of it your eyes will be opened, and you will be like God, knowing good and evil."*

If the serpent was only an unfamiliar external entity, surely this direct contradiction would have been met with greater skepticism. But if it was a projection of the internal emerging voice of the conscious self, then it makes the ready acceptance of this contradiction more realistic. We are more at ease with weighing up possibilities within ourselves, even contradictory options, and instantly changing our minds from one to the other. It also explains the silence of Ish. Maybe a similar conversation was developing in him which in turn prepared him to simply accept the fruit, without question, once it was offered. Let's look at the text again:

> *"You will not die; for God knows that when you eat of it your eyes will be opened, and you will be like God, knowing good and evil."*

As with all great temptations, there is some truth in it. God does indeed know good and evil, but the motivation behind the prohibition is falsely presented. These words imply that God is prohibiting them from eating the fruit because he does not want to share this knowledge or likeness with them. The very nature of God is misrepresented as one withholding what they are lacking. This is a fundamental misunderstanding of God. This sense of lack-of-being is then used to suggest the desirability of the fruit.

Why would the earthlings be so susceptible to a sense of lack? Every child is born into a world where everyone around him/her is bigger and allowed to do more. Growing up amongst others who are stronger and have fewer limitations than you creates an ideal environment in which desire becomes twisted into covetousness. It is easy to desire the being of the other if your own seems so insignificant. And so it becomes normal for children to continually push the boundaries, to attempt to do what the others do, to reach for the fruit that is prohibited. Why do parents prohibit us from things that they partake of? This confusion of good and bad imitation can easily translate into rivalry and conflict. And conflict can escalate into violence. This violence is not limited to the physical - it is any attempt to take from another what you think you lack in yourself. If the imagery of a fall is valid, it is valid in this sense. A fundamental misinterpretation has taken place. Instead of the gratuitous givenness of existence, a sense of lack became the filter through which reality is interpreted. Consequently, much of desire becomes twisted into an acquisitive type that attempts to fill the imagined void by grasping.

GRASPING FOR THE GIFT

In this context, it is relevant to consider whether God, in some way, partakes of the knowledge of good and evil/bad. Does God differentiate between love and hate? Is God indifferent to a child being abused? The rest of the Scriptures make it clear that there are things God is for and things God is against. But we don't have to look further than verse 22 to see that God indeed knows good and evil: "*Then the Lord God said, 'See, the man has become like one of us, knowing good and evil.'*" However, it was not through a process of misunderstanding, a sense of lack-of-being and twisted desire, that God came to acquire such knowledge. Was there another way for humanity to acquire such knowledge? Yes, there was! It was always God's intention for us to grow into the full reality of his own image and likeness - a likeness that includes the wisdom of making value judgments. The problem here is not so much the *ends* but the *means*. In our haste we grasped for what we were not able to contain.

A memory from my childhood illustrates this point. I was about seven years of age and it was a week before Christmas. My two brothers and I were playfully guessing what our gifts might be, when my dad informed us that the gifts were already bought and our speculations could not change them. Obviously we wanted to know what they were and if perhaps we might just look at them … from a distance. "No, you must wait until Christmas day to open your gifts and play with them" said my mother. It was only a matter of time. But time is what I did not have much patience for. One afternoon I searched through a cupboard in my parents' room and found it! The gifts weren't wrapped yet and I quickly figured out which one was meant for me. Carefully I opened the box with a battery-powered motorbike. The next hour was pure bliss discovering all the functions and noises my new toy had. At the end of this stolen playtime, I put everything back as best I could. For a couple of days I sneaked into their room and went through the same ritual.

However, when one afternoon my mom began wrapping the gifts, she realized what had happened. When I heard her call my name, my heart sank for I knew, she knew. A severe reprimand followed.

Christmas day came and my two brothers and I were given our gifts. Theirs were wrapped but mine was not. My parents handed each child their gift, starting with the eldest. What delight as they observed each boy's surprise and joy. Mine was handed to me last but in reality it was no longer a gift. I tried to look surprised, but nothing could change the fact that I took what was suppose to be given and thereby invalidated the gift. Desire without patience becomes twisted.

Twisting of Desire

Notice that before the serpent's suggestion, no desire is expressed by the woman. But after the suggestion, *"the woman saw that the tree was good for food, and that it was a delight to the eyes, and that the tree was to be desired to make one wise."* Desire does not spontaneously erupt between the woman and the fruit but is mediated by a conversation with another. In this case, it might well be an internal other; nevertheless, there is a mediation.

The process of mimetic desire is not evil in itself. However, when desire originates from a sense of lack, it becomes twisted and acquisitive. And for such a sense of lack to exist, a rival is suggested - in this case, a god who is withholding. Remember, God expressed desire in the creation of mankind, but it was not a sense of lack that motivated that desire. Desire can have another type of origin - the divine type - where it is the super-abundance, the sense-of-fullness that energizes the kind of desire that gives itself to another.

...she took of its fruit and ate; and she also gave some to her husband, who was with her, and he ate.

Again, it is in reflective relationship that this creative process, whereby the embryonic self is birthed, is completed. We do not become human in isolation but in relationship. This is true in both a positive and negative sense.

Then the eyes of both were opened, and they knew that they were naked; and they sewed fig leaves together and made loincloths for themselves.

They were naked previously, but now they know it. Individual wills and personalities were not completely formed before and consequently, in that union, there was nothing to hide. However, once self-consciousness is formed, a separation takes place between self and all else. Ish no longer experiences himself as part of Isha or part of God. This process of separation contains within itself inevitable guilt. I am no longer part of the flow but an independent actor that may cause things to happen. This initial realization of cause and effect is overwhelming. Everything happens because of me! An understanding of chance and the appreciation that other actors also cause things will take time.

Let's think of this in historical terms. The development of con-sciousness in early humans happened within community. Group identity and group consciousness were more essential than indi-vidual consciousness. Such group unity was an absolute necessity for survival. The gradual separation of the independent ego within a group also created an ideal environment for guilt. To assert one's individuality within a group that gave and sustained your very existence would have been traumatic. Today still it is a traumatic experience to separate yourself from a group that has been an intimate part of your life.

Just as the earthlings were naked before, but did not know it, they were also mortal before but did not fully appreciate the reality of death. Now they do. Death consciousness enters and the fear of death, the drive to preserve self, will be the cause of untold suffering. What is the difference between an animalistic instinct to survive and human death-consciousness? Physical danger is an occasional reality, and all animals deal with it in the moment. However, a self founded on a sense of lack-of-being perceives danger everywhere and naturally inflames rivalry with anyone who seems to have what it lacks. Self-preservation in this context becomes amplified because it is not only concerned with occasional physical danger but with an ever-present insecure self. Whatever questions the value or meaning of this insecure self, is perceived as a danger.

GOD FROM THE PERSPECTIVE OF THE FEARFUL

They heard the sound of the Lord God walking in the garden at the time of the evening breeze, and the man and his wife hid themselves from the presence of the Lord God among the trees of the garden. But the Lord God called to the man, and said to him, "Where are you?" He said, "I heard the sound of you in the garden, and I was afraid, because I was naked; and I hid myself." He said, "Who told you that you were naked? Have you eaten from the tree of which I commanded you not to eat?" The man said, "The woman whom you gave to be with me, she gave me fruit from the tree, and I ate." Then the Lord God said to the woman,

"What is this that you have done?" The woman said, "The serpent tricked me, and I ate."

- Genesis 3:8-13

The newly formed independent self is suddenly obsessed with the sensory information that connects it to a reality apart from itself. Desire has given priority to sensory knowledge and the text itself has now taken on this perspective: *"they heard the sound of God," "God walking in the garden," "the cool of the day."* For the first time, the character of God now enters the drama in a sensory way, as if the text itself is now written from the perspective of the earthlings who have partaken of this sensual knowledge. The implications for how we interpret the story from here onwards are enormous, for we are not dealing with an independent perspective but with the limited view of the earthlings - Ish and Isha. That the text is now written from their point of view is confirmed as they heard: *"God called to the man[earthling) 'Where are you?'"*

On this point, Sandor Goodhart writes:

[I}s the image of God that the text projects for us, an image based upon the distorted perspective of the characters within it, characters who have experienced something they are unhappy about and that colors their perspective of things?[5]

This new dimension to the text opens up amazing possibilities. We cannot read and ignore the perspective we are dealing with. The narrative tells us something, but the very structure of the narrative is subjective. What it says about God and the events to follow are all subjective descriptions of the characters who have discovered themselves naked, afraid and ashamed. In this atmosphere of fear, it is easy to see God as retributive and punishing.

Every child needs to deal with the fact that the same parents who provide also seem to take away at times. Sometimes they say 'yes' and other times they say 'no.' Parents enable us but also limit us. The perspective that develops after the earthlings partake of this confusion of knowledge, the knowledge of good and evil, is similar to the perspective of a child that imagines his parents as both providing and punishing. If we are indeed dealing with a child's perspective then the implications are significant. And what can be said about a child's perspective, can also be said of humanity in its infancy.

BEING HUMAN AND PROJECTING BLAME

When confronted by God, the man blames God and the woman. The woman in turn blames the snake and in effect the God who created this snake. The process of projecting our guilt and scape-goating others begins. Remember we are dealing with an emerging conscious self, and in these early stages many decisions have to be made about what is part of me and what is not. To separate oneself from guilt and project it outside oneself brings immediate relief. It is, however, not a permanent solution.

To the woman he said,

"I will greatly increase your pangs in childbearing;

in pain you shall bring forth children,

yet your desire shall be for your husband,

and he shall rule over you."

And to the man he said,

"Because you have listened to the voice of your wife,

and have eaten of the tree

about which I commanded you,

    'You shall not eat of it,'

cursed is the ground because of you;

    in toil you shall eat of it all the days of your life;

thorns and thistles it shall bring forth for you;

    and you shall eat the plants of the field.

By the sweat of your face

    you shall eat bread

until you return to the ground,

    for out of it you were taken;

you are dust,

    and to dust you shall return."

- Genesis 3:16-19 RSV

The pronouncement of the curses by God is often seen as punishment, but everything that is said is also consistent with the natural progression from infancy to adulthood. As such the pronouncements can be seen as God simply stating the consequences of partaking of the fruit, the reality of becoming fully human. Toddlers might enjoy the naked bliss of bumping into other naked friends without any painful consequences. But for an adult woman the consequence is most probably painful childbearing. Children might live in the self-sufficient paradise in which food is effortlessly provided for them, but adults eat through the sweat and effort they exert.

This is not a process God tried to prevent. Everything was set up by God in such a way as to make it possible. The prohibition itself seems to have been necessary to awaken desire and set the process in motion.

> *The man named his wife Eve, because she was the mother of all living. And the Lord God made garments of skins for the man and for his wife, and clothed them.*
>
> *- Genesis 3:20-21 RSV*

It is only after facing God's pronouncement of what life would be like from then on, that Adam names Eve: "*The man called his wife's name Eve, because she was the mother of all living*" (3:20). Why the mother of all life? Logically she would only be the mother of human life. But for Adam she has opened up a whole new world and as such a whole new life.

Zornberg beautifully describes the significance of this naming of Eve as follows:

> *In naming her in this way, he marks a passionate and ambiguous knowledge that he can express only with the baffled intensity of one who has stepped into a transformed world ... Eve has brought Adam into a world of uncertainty and agitation, of process and risk— "beyond the grasp of his intellect." His sovereign relation to his world and its meanings yields to her enigmatic vitality: "The essence of life flows to him from her." She has proven irreducibly other, an otherness he experiences as intense life. The way he now uses language to name her contains the irony, the doubleness, the revelation of poetry. She takes him beyond himself, and he*

strains to communicate this transcendence. In a word, Eve has seduced Adam. One effect of seduction is to move the other to speechlessness, and then into a new, dazzled language. [6]

Are we beginning to recognize these earthlings as fully human? Yes! It is very significant that up to this stage nothing is said about sin or a fall. Yes, God announces the consequences of their actions, but none of their actions are declared to be sin. And yes, in the final act of this drama Adam and Eve are expelled from Eden. However, this image is not one of a vertical fall, but more suggestive of giving birth. Human consciousness with all its complexities is birthed out of the naive innocence of childhood, the unconscious paradise, into the richness of a more complex reality.

Growing Up

Then the Lord God said, "See, the man has become like one of us, knowing good and evil."

- Genesis 3:22 RSV

Could it be that this verse means what it plainly says? Could it be that it is exactly the humans who partook of the knowledge of good and bad, who have developed a self capable of making value judgments, who are more like God than those who lived in the paradise of naive innocence? Maybe the project of creating humans in the image and likeness of God was not an instant act but one that required a process. And neither was this process forced upon us but, rather, God creates a garden of possibilities, seduces us into it, gives us extravagant freedom, even the freedom to disobey, and then invites us to participate in the creative process of becoming.

"...and now, he might reach out his hand and take also from the tree of life, and eat, and live forever"— therefore the Lord God sent him forth from the garden of Eden, to till the ground from which he was taken. He drove out the man; and at the east of the garden of Eden he placed the cherubim, and a sword flaming and turning to guard the way to the tree of life.

- *Genesis 3:22-24 RSV*

Why prevent humanity from becoming immortal? Maybe this early stage of consciousness is not a state in which we should continue forever. It is unlikely that humanity would ponder the meaning of time and self with any urgency, if the limit of death was removed. Immortality might also have been seen as a quick fix, a way to instantly and magically return to the less complex, timeless, and peaceful state of the pre-ego unconscious.

However beautiful this pre-conscious stage of life is, however delightful this shameless nakedness seems to us, this naive innocence cannot be compared to the depth of intimacy enjoyed by adult lovers. Yes, as we grow we become more self-conscious, we develop personal borders and we have to negotiate the complexities of another independent will, but when the borders are finally crossed there is a fulfilled joy not present in the blissful ignorance of toddlers.

There might yet be a way for the earthlings to partake of the tree of life, but there is no way to undo the emergence of self-consciousness. To prevent them from desperately grasping at the tree of life the way they grasped at the fruit from the tree of the knowledge of good and evil, a more permanent solution is required. It will involve facing this new harsher reality of navigating the complexities of relationship that involve parties with independent wills. And an awareness of the inevitability of death, would focus the search for meaning. It will require their new-found capacity to make value judgments to mature so that, eventually, they will come to repentance - a transformation of the entire person.

Endnotes

1   Charlesworth, James H. *The Good and Evil Serpent: How a Universal Symbol Became Christianized.* New Haven: Yale University Press, 2010.

2   Neumann, Erich. *The Origins And History Of Consciousness*: Volume 118 (International Library of Psychology) (p. 10). Taylor and Francis. Kindle Edition.

3   ibid. (p. 276).

4   Ricoeur, Paul. *The Symbolism of Evil.* Boston: Beacon Press, 1967. p 256

5   Goodhart, Sandor. *The Prophetic Law*, page 110, Kindle Edition

6   Zornberg, Avivah Gottlieb. *The Murmuring Deep: Reflections on the Biblical Unconscious* (p. 24). Knopf Doubleday Publishing Group. Kindle Edition.

CHAPTER SIX

Origins Reimagined

To unravel a thread from a tapestry could ruin the whole fabric. It would be much wiser to leave the thread where it is and just color it differently, or surround it by other threads that obscure it. Sometimes our stories develop in such a way that everything becomes new - even the beginning needs to be re-imagined. But deeply embedded stories can't easily be removed. To reframe them, and consequently to reinterpret them, would be a wiser strategy. And that's partly the strategy of Genesis 1. It reframes the Yahwist creation narratives in a way that transforms their meaning.

Development in Consciousness

Genesis 1 represents a radically new understanding of God, creation, and humanity. It was authored after Genesis 2 and 3 (Yahwist) and the source behind this text is known as the Priestly Source - P for short. As such it also represents a later development in thought. By that I do not mean that it developed solely from the Yahwist source but rather that various influences pushed the narrative forward. By placing this later developed narrative before the Yahwist accounts of creation, it completely reframed those earlier stories.

The prominence of the conscious mind in the Genesis 1 narrative is evident in that unconscious symbolism is fading. There are no talking animals, no magical trees, no speculative metaphors that could encourage the superstitions that were so abundant in ancient religions. The symbolism of the unconscious contains a beautiful wisdom, but when it is given free rein it easily develops into unhelpful superstitions and hyper-spirituality. This does not mean that the wisdom of the unconscious is completely absent here. Rather, as with the development of humans, the unconscious becomes obscured.

And so Genesis 1 represents a development in consciousness. It is an exploration of origins that opens up new horizons not imagined by the previous stories. The scope is no longer terrestrial, as in the earlier Yahwist creation story, but cosmic. Neither does this creation story begin somewhere within time, but rather time itself comes into existence in the poetic rhythm of this narrative as day follows night and each new day builds upon what came before.

Consciousness of Time and Narrative

Greater awareness of time and the sequence of events is entirely consistent with a more developed consciousness. The conscious is separating itself from the unconscious, and the new understanding that is awakened can be likened to the light separating itself from darkness (verse 3).

But what is this new awareness of time? In the unconscious state, the sequence of events is not that important. When everything is one and all is whole, the relationships between separate entities are invisible for there are no separate entities. But with the awakening of a separate self, the separation of all things becomes visible and so also the temporal relationships that connect them. Time becomes the space in which dynamic relationship exists.

All of reality is in motion. Everything is in the process of being changed. Every sentence in Genesis 1 bears witness to this truth.

Time is a movement, a movement with a shape. But what is this shape?

Some think time is a line; a line with a direction; an arrow - always moving forward from what was, to what is yet to be. And there is no way to reverse its direction, no going back and no stopping the future. Yet, many things from the past return. Does time twirl around in circles like the circular serpent? From spring to summer to autumn to winter, round and round our planet spins, and so too our lives. This circular movement could be good ... or not. The rhythms help us remember and help us learn. What dies in the winter makes space for new life. But ... the patterns become familiar; the routines and habits carve out a path, a circular path, that soon becomes a trench in which many have lost hope of ever being able to escape.

So what is it - are we moving anywhere new, or are we trapped in the boringly predictable cycles of time? Is there anything new?

But what if the shape of time is a spiral! A spiral has both rhythm and direction: a repetitious cycle and a forward trajectory. It is moving somewhere, yet it does not lose the beauty of its pattern. Each repetition is unique and its forward motion retains the memory of its past. Day follows night, and night follows day, yet each day offers something new although it is similar to days gone by.

It is in this rhythmic motion, in this unfolding narrative itself, that God has made himself at home. This is the beautiful new vision presented by the first chapter of Genesis. All of creation is his temple and the whole story is permeated with his presence. In humans a unique opportunity exists to reflect this presence, for the story to become aware and conscious of itself.

DIVINE PRESENCE

The general theme remains theological, as in earlier texts, in that it explores similar questions such as: Who and what is God? Where is God? And what is the relation between God and creation, specifically the relation between God and humans?

It also asks, where is God at rest? What kind of resting place does he desire? This was a key theme for early religion. Both the garden and the temple were images that were primarily concerned with an appropriate space for God to rest in. The temple was not so much a place where people went to worship as it was a space in which the divine was at home. During a time when each tribe and nation claimed that a god chose their mountain, their city, and their temple as a special abode, Genesis 1 envisions a whole new space in which God dwells. In the crescendo of this story, God finds rest, not in an isolated temple or a hidden garden, but in the goodness of creation itself.

TOHU WA-BOHU

When God began to create heaven and earth, and the earth then was welter and waste [tohu wa-bohu] and darkness over the deep[Tehom] and God's breath hovering over the waters.

- Genesis 1:1-2 RA

When God began creating ... there was something already present: Chaos! What a peculiar thought. In fact, this idea is so perplexing that volumes of theories would be written to explain it away and to justify us overlooking the chaos of verse 2 and hastily skipping to verse 3. It would have been so much simpler if God began creating by commanding "let there be light." But there it is, right in the middle of God beginning to create and the first creative words spoken - chaos. Before a word is spoken, Elohim broods upon this depth of the unformed. What is happening here? At the very moment of creation, the *ruach Elohim*, the divine movements, vibrate upon the face of a chaotic depth.

But Rashi, a 10th century Rabbi, translated this verse as follows:

At the beginning of the creation of heaven and earth when the earth was without form and void and there was darkness ... God said Let there be...

His argument, which many translators are now supporting, is that *the beginning* is a subordinate clause to the act of creation that begins when God speaks. In other words Genesis 1:1 is not the first act of creation but rather it is in verse 3 where God speaks for the first time. It seems that chaos is the raw material from which the created order emerges.

Why has it been easier to imagine God creating out of nothing than God creating out of this chaotic depth? What is it about chaos that has evokes disgust and inspires fear? Since the earliest myths humans told, chaos has been associated with crisis, with evil, and with monstrous destruction. Our experience of chaos is seldom pleasant. Rather, we associate it with things falling apart, with confusion and with destruction. As such it became the enemy - the dragon that devours. And this mythic understanding of chaos has certainly found allies in some forms of Christian theology. Karl Barth, for instance, describes the chaos as that which God negated, worse than nothing, from which nothing good can come.[1]

Could it be that the author of Genesis is beginning to subvert the myth of chaos? Have we misunderstood the tohu wa-bohu? Maybe we have feared it the way we fear the unconscious. We avoid this depth for it does not subject itself to control; it does not follow the patterns of our conscious logic. And if God is only perceived from the perspective of the conscious self, then we imagine a God of control, of mastery and of order - not a God in relationship with chaos. Like Jacob, we have no desire for the untamed wildness of Esau. We want a God as ordered, civilized, self-sufficient and conscious as ourselves. We would rather run and pretend that Esau does not exist than acknowledge this relation to the untamed other.

But God is more than what we can fit into our conscious frame-works. He is more than what is known and ordered. This God is present too in the unknown, the unordered, the unformed, the unexplained, the unpredictable and the unconscious. This God is not obliged to validate our order or submit to our reason. Yes, a distinction is made between Elohim and tohu wa-bohu, but God shows no aversion to it. Rather, there seems to be a mysterious attraction. Is there a part in God over which God exerts no control? Could chaos, in similar fashion as Esau, be a relation rather than an enemy? We seldom stand amazed in front of the expected order, rather it is unexpected chaos that astounds us. The kind of order in which chaos is an enemy, becomes oppressive, manipulating and ever more rigid. It soon loses whatever semblance of beauty it had. The only way in which order can retain its beauty is by embracing chaos as a friend. This kind of order acknowledges that it originates in and is composed of chaos. And it is in nurturing this playful relationship that new meaning, new beauty, and renewed order is possible.

Those who study these ancient texts have noticed the similarities between the first few verses of Genesis and the myth of Enuma Elish. In fact the very meaning of the words Enuma Elish is: "When in the beginning," an almost identical starting line to the first verse of Genesis. The connections become even more astounding as we follow the story further. In this myth it is the chaotic waters, personified in the female face of Tiamat, that need to be overcome by the violent evil wind of Marduk. In Genesis we have chaotic waters, we have a wind, and we also have a face upon these waters. What we translated as "the face of the deep" is in Hebrew "the face of Tehom" - the Hebrew equivalent to Tiamat. In the Hebrew language it lacks the definitive article 'the' and therefore is used as a proper name ("The face of Tehom" vs "The face of the Tehom").

Do you recognize the unconscious matrix of the text? The Genesis creation account is written over the unconscious text of many myths. The same signifiers are present, but the meaning is transformed as new relationships are formed between these signifiers. The God of Genesis does not need violence to defeat an evil formless chaos; rather his breath silently hovers, whispering possibilities of beauty and life. Can we recognize what it is within this formless depth that attracts the spirit of Elohim? The tohu wa-bohu is more than the opposite of order - it's a different kind of order. It is more than nothing, it's the possibility of everything.

Remember, this watery depth is not the seas, for they were created on the third day. The book of Job perceives this depth as a watery womb from which the seas were born.

Who hedged the sea with double doors, when it gushed forth from the womb. when I made cloud its clothing, and thick mist its swaddling bands?

- Job 38:8-9 RA

CREATIVE EDGE OF CHAOS

In the Hebrew Bible tohu is used to describe the desolate desert. The bohu is closely associated - a poetic twin (welter and waste) - and also refers to the uninhabitable nature of this wilderness. One Midrashic commentary translates it as "bewildered and astonished."[2] And in the Kabbalah, an ancient Jewish tradition of mystical interpretation, it is compared to Yesod hapashut ("simple element"), in which "everything is united as one, without differentiation."[3]

The compound *tohu wa-bohu* has more meaning than the individual parts. It adds a poetic rhythm; a repetition that introduces a slight variation; a nuanced meaning; a differentiating note. And as such, these reverberations harmonize with the vibrating wind (ruach) - the spirit that hovers over the waters.

Creation does not begin with self-sufficient power or authoritative words, but with a wordless hovering. It is in this contemplative silence that the possibilities within the chaos begin to dance. Tohu wa-bohu - a poetic echo in the silence: Elusive messages drifting; unlikely possibilities awakening; signifiers rearranging. With each repetition of tohu wa-bohu the surface grows more unstable. Possibilities vibrate. What might be nothing, murmurs of what might yet be something. And within the formless, patterns emerge. Creation is not the result of an enforced design but a willing response to divine seduction.

Tohu wa-bohu - these fluctuations intertwine with the movements of Elohim.

A breath, a whisper - and the depth begins to pulsate.

Suddenly the murmur finds its voice.

The surface of the concealment opens.

Light was hidden within the darkness, but now it is revealed.

These scattered messages might yet have meaning.

The in-distinction contains distinction.

The vibrations sift them apart.

There is a deep, deep pattern within the chaos, and with each differentiating echo the background noise finds a rhythm. This primordial drum-beat might yet be a symphony.

And God said... such simple clarity.

This voice was born from the endless echoes, the deep, deep yearnings of an abyss. Even at the heart of what is formless, there is a whisper of what is possible. This voice is not in conflict with the formless noise, neither does this order violate the chaos. Rather, it gives voice to its yearnings and draws forth its beauty.

And God said ... and it was so.

The echoes in the deep reverberate to the surface and burst into creative voice.

The word and the act are one: *"And God said... and it was so."*

Does the word precede the act of creation? Or does the process of creation give God a voice?

Elohim - the infinite possibility of everything - is actualized in part.

And so, in the first five days of creation, word and creative action flow together without any pause: And God said ... and it was so. A new order emerges from the chaos.

But then... a new difference comes into play - life.

Then God said, "Let the sea swarm forth with swarming creatures" (1:20).

This is not the manipulative command of an autocrat, but the whisper of love, luring its creation, enticing her to bring forth the life and beauty that is latent in her. Creation happens not as an independent act of dominance but rather as a letting be. Again we see a God who makes creation possible, instead of than one who manipulates everything according to a predefined design. This God does not control the narrative but is the framework that makes meaning possible.

Another surprise… the crescendo of this symphony:

> And God said, "Let us make a human in our image, by our likeness, to hold sway over the fish of the sea and the fowl of the heavens and the cattle and the wild beasts and all the crawling things that crawl upon the earth."

> And God created the human in his image, in the image of God He created him, male and female He created them.

> - Genesis 1:26-27 RA

No longer is it a case of "And God said … and it was so."

The seamless flow of word to action stops. A pause. A hesitation - an unstable fluctuation. A deeper echo interrupts the simple flow and from its center, a desire pulsates. The echo hears itself. From the unconscious potentiality, consciousness erupts. A new complexity is born in these words as language becomes self-reflective: "Let Us make man in Our image, according to Our likeness."

It is this complex, echoing, self-reflective quality that is a unique aspect of human consciousness. The unformed possibility, the incomprehensible multiplicity that is Elohim, will be reflected in this being. Even the immeasurable depth of chaos will find a home in this new order. This new instantiation of consciousness will embody more than an instinctual echo - humanity will embody the unstable fluctuation from which untold possibilities could erupt.

In the creation of everything else, God could still be misidentified as a solitary entity acting upon a separate creation. But in the creation of humanity, the relational and reflective nature of God is revealed in the conversation with us - "Let Us." Both the unity and multiplicity of God is revealed here. And this quality would be reflected in the creation of human consciousness, which is both a unified singular 'I' but consists of multiple relationships and voices. A desire is expressed within this relationship and it is in the creation of humanity where desire will find resonance.

If this primal chaos is not evil, not an enemy of God, but rather part of the process by which God creates, then this passage has great relevance to our present lives. For none of us began in a perfectly ordered and tranquil world. Neither is our internal world without chaos.

But it is in the middle of this mess, in the heart of chaos, that this God does his best work. In the midst of darkness there is a light that has not been snuffed out, a hope against hope, a grace that keeps pouring itself out into our existence. If we listen we can hear the whisper of desire saying: *something truly new and beautiful is possible for you.* This formless abyss can swarm with life. The illogical fragments, the residue of uninterpreted messages and repressed desires can be brought together in meaningful fulfillment. God is in this place … in this I, I did not know.

Compared to the Yahwist narratives of Genesis 2 and 3, we can appreciate that there is both a continuation of the same themes and a development of those concepts. What is not always obvious, especially if one reads Genesis 1 to 3 as one progressive story, is that there are marked differences.

New Framing & Unintended Consequences

Throughout Genesis 1 we have seen a beautiful synergy between the creative unconscious and the logic of the conscious. The imaginative aspects of the story have been combined with the logical in such a way that it is no longer illusionary. And because of that, the imaginary unconscious aspects of the story have become more truthful and beautiful. Similarly, the reasonableness of the conscious, the sequence of time, and the rhythmic control with which the story was consciously constructed, have been enriched through the poetic creativity of the unconscious.

Because of the striking different level of consciousness with which Genesis 1 was written compared to the Yahwist accounts, some think it was a deliberate effort to correct some of the Yahwist ideas.[4] If some of the ideas presented by the Yahwist makes you uncomfortable, you are not alone.

It is possible that the author/s, known as P, also found some of the theological positions questionable and set about to correct them. Genesis 1 - 2:4 reframes the Yahwist (J) origin stories in such a way as to change many of its assumptions. Whether or not this was one of the goals of P, it is clear that how we understand Genesis 1 greatly influences the way we interpret the Yahwist narratives that follow.

One of the ways in which Genesis 1 is interpreted, places undue emphasis on God's sovereign control. Some of these interpreters think that P purposely set out to correct some of J's theology. The idea of a naive deity who progressively learns and improves creation was unacceptable. P, therefore, portrays God as perfectly in control as he goes about intentionally creating exactly what he purposed. Each act of creation (except for two) is followed by the proclamation: It is good. There are no surprises, no errors, no unforeseen consequences. Even the creation of humanity includes both male and female (1:27) in one act.

Reading Genesis 1 as a display of God's mastery and control has had a huge influence on how the subsequent chapters were understood. For if God is perfect and all he creates is in accordance with his perfect design, then creation itself would have been perfectly good as well. It is, however, obvious to every human who ever lived that not all of creation is perfectly good. So what happened? This conundrum creates a new context in which to interpret the Yahwist creation myths. Instead of it being the story of what-makes-us-human, it now becomes the story of what-went-wrong. The garden becomes a historic deathless paradise - the original perfection for which we were designed. And the process by which we become human, able to make value judgments, is now interpreted as a fall from the state of perfection.

The Yahwist story is transformed from a creative exploration of what makes us human to a legendary lost paradise for which we now nostalgically long. Because humanity is seen as the crescendo of creation in Genesis 1, the garden in Genesis 2 is re-interpreted as an abode made for humanity, instead of a divine dwelling in which humans are placed for the purpose of growth. Although P reframes the creation event and introduces many beautiful insights, it may also obscure the original thought of the Yahwist account.

Yet the complexities inherent in the development of the text add new dimensions of meaning. In it we can recognize people like ourselves trying to make sense of their existence ... but we can also recognize the whisper of our Abba, the spirit that hovers over the seemingly chaotic waters of our minds, drawing forth new form, new concepts, and new meaning.

Endnotes

1   *Church Dogmatics* III.1.105

2   Midrash Rabbah: *Genesis, Volume One,* translated by Rabbi Dr. H. Freedman; London: Soncino Press, 1983; ISBN 0-900689-38-2; p. 15.

3   Chaim Kramer, *Anatomy of the Soul,* Breslov Research Institute, Jerusalem/New York City 1998 ISBN 0-930213-51-3

4   Batto, Bernard F. *In the Beginning: Essays on Creation Motifs in the Bible and the Ancient Near East.* P 85. Winona Lake: Eisenbrauns, 2014.

CHAPTER SEVEN

Beautiful Questions

The way we have interpreted the Genesis texts in the previous chapters might have been new, even perplexing, for some. It is certainly not the way I initially understood their message. Thinking through the implications will take time, but let's explore some of the possibilities that have opened up.

Many of the concepts that were so fundamental to my early faith have been inverted, even subverted. What is "original perfection," and what is it not? Are the events described here actual historical events? Does the concept of a fall even make sense anymore? How does this affect other areas of theology and our understanding of what Jesus came to accomplish?

Original Perfection?

The archetypal memory inherited by every person, together with the experience repeated in every individual's development of self-consciousness, makes the intuition of an original perfection particularly strong.

To summarize: before the full emergence of a separate self, there is only an undifferentiated oneness. This experience of paradise in which all contradiction lies side by side, in which neither time nor death exists, is a state of consciousness that begins before the formation of self-consciousness. These experiences are inscribed in the unconscious and communicated to the conscious through symbols and intuitions.

The meaning of these subliminal messages are not immediately clear, for they do not follow the same rules as our conscious language. They need translation and interpretation. This might be why we so readily grasp for interpretations of origin stories that presume to be historical fact. For if the messages and enigmatic symbols we receive from the unconscious are given a concrete history, they fit right in with the ordered conscious mind. We eagerly embrace the simplicity of a sequential and logical story rather than the laborious task of developing better relations with the unconscious. Instead of exploring and giving meaning to these unconscious messages, we can simply receive a ready-made neat explanation.

However, as mentioned before, this awareness of union is not simply the naive misunderstanding of an undeveloped mind, but an authentic participation in reality. Although the conscious mind will bring a recognition of the separation between entities, there remains an underlying unity. According to the author of Colossians, Christ is nothing less than the one in whom all things consist (1:17).

Maybe this yearning for perfection is more than a memory of our undivided pre-conscious state but a recognition that we have always been part of a movement that is whole. And this story is given a whole new meaning in the person of Jesus who holds it all together, from beginning to end, in himself (16). He is the source, the sustainer, and the seducer of all that is. All things exist through him, for him, and towards him. It seems that this perfection and wholeness is full of relational movement. Christ reveals that it was always God's beautiful intention that we should be blameless before him (22) and given every opportunity to grow, develop, and be strengthened (10-12) to receive, contain, and retain the fullness of God (2:9-10).

ACTUAL HISTORY?

So is the Genesis account actual history? For many, this is a crucial question. In a way, we could consider this archetypal memory as based on real historical events. The numerous tribes and groups that emerged into full self-consciousness have similar symbols and stories to describe that traumatic event. The story of Adam and Eve can, therefore, be seen as this collective archetypal memory of real events. However, it is not factual history in the sense we have developed historic writing in the past few hundred years. There never was a time where snakes could speak and magical trees could impart wisdom through consuming its fruit. Looking at the broader literary context in which these stories evolved, it is obvious that myth is a literary genre of its own and should not be forced into our later developed genre of historical writing. It is as likely that a snake spoke as it is that Adapa broke the wing of the south wind god.

These are metaphors. Yet, the story is true. True in that it is the story of you and me and of every human being who ever lived. Each one of us developed from pre-conscious babies through different stages of consciousness. Each one of us encountered whispering voices that suggested a lack of being, a sense of inadequacy. Each one of us grasped for what promised fulfillment. These stories are partly conscious constructs of unconscious memories. As such they combine the logic and sequence of the conscious with the symbols of the unconscious in a density of text that cries out for continued interpretation. To simply accept the kind of interpretation that reduces the text to static historical events is both lazy and detrimental to the ongoing exploration of meaning.

What are the implications of interpreting these texts as historical?

If there once was a perfect world and a perfect humanity, but we are presently faced with a lesser world and a humanity that is fallen, then it is easy to develop a nostalgic longing for that original utopia. Consequently, some strains of theology still long to recover that original perfection, that faultless design of what life was supposed to be. Truth is sought in an imagined unspoiled beginning.

When we construct our own stories in the context of this idea of a lost perfection, then it becomes so easy to miss the beauty and value of the present. The meta-narrative of the fall by implication means that our current world is less than it was supposed to be… that you are less than what was originally planned. This nostalgic longing for an imagined paradise goes hand in hand with a sense of lack regarding the here and now.

The idea that everything was historically complete and perfect in the beginning has an impact on many other areas of theology. For example, the doctrine of salvation becomes overly obsessed with a conquest to recover this origin. Consequently, the mission of Jesus is reduced to redeeming this original design. But what is the alternative?

CREATION EX NIHILO OR EX PROFUNDIS?

The ideas of a historical perfect deathless paradise, original sin, and the consequent fall are each deeply connected with how we understand creation. And our understanding of creation is inseparably linked to our concept of a Creator. If we imagine a Creator completely separate from creation, independently acting with absolute control and without any interference while creating, then it follows logically that such a creation would display the goodness and perfection of its Creator. To a large extent, it was ideas about God's sovereign power, his complete otherness, and his absolute control that shaped the many varieties of creation doctrines. From this perspective, whatever imperfections we observe in creation cannot be the result of this original act of creation, but must be due to some subsequent event, namely the fall.

It is unlikely that the author or the audience of Genesis 1 were as obsessed about the material origins of the universe as later theological speculators. Much more likely would be their interest in the way God creates. And our main interest here is more in the creation of meaning and the relationship between Creator and creation, than in the material origins of the universe. The philosophical prominence of creation ex nihilo - creation out of nothing - despite the fact that

Genesis does not make one reference to it, should give us pause to ponder. *The theologian doth protest too much, methinks.*

There is much in the philosophy of creation ex nihilo that is beautiful and with which I wholeheartedly agree. I can affirm, for instance, that God is indeed the ground of all existence. Yet these statements of beauty should not blind us to the more sinister aspects of the doctrine. The desire for a God of sovereign power, who is in absolute control, who needs nothing and no one to accomplish his will, could also be a projection of our own perverse desire for independence and dominance. It could be that we have misunderstood what true power looks like and that this misunderstanding is at the heart of much of the doctrine of creation ex nihilo. God's power as revealed in Jesus is not the power of mastery and dominance but the power of persuasion and love. Should this understanding not be more influential in our description of creation? Catherine Keller presents a beautifully poetic and more thorough treatment of this topic in her book, "*The Face of the Deep.*"[1]

If we do honor the Genesis text, then surely we should appreciate that the creation narrative does not mention "nothing" at all, but it does mention many other "things," including tohu wa-bohu, the watery deep, the face of this deep, the movements of ruach, and Elohim. Could it be that the Creator is more relational than what is imagined in the doctrine of creation ex nihilo? Could it be that here, in the Genesis origin stories, the author's intuition of a complex, even chaotic relationship is an inspired insight into what would later become known as trinity. Trinity, after all, is an attempt to name the complexity of relationship inherent to God.

The alternative to *creation ex nihilo* is *creation ex profundis* - the profound depth of possibilities of Genesis 1:2. From the perspective of creation ex profundis, creation itself participates in its own creation. Both God, for whom all things are possible, and creation, which realizes those possibilities, are active participants in the ongoing event of creation. The God of love does not control the process or the narrative, but influences, seduces, and calls us forward towards the greater good and beauty that is possible. We are co-creators, invited to become the very display of God's image and likeness in this world. But this also means that from the very start of creation, it is a journey towards fulfilling the possibilities in God. This story does not begin with a perfect creation, but a journey of realizing the inexhaustible possibilities in God.

All around us we observe a pregnant creation. The difficult times of pain throughout the world are simply birth pangs. But it's not only around us; it's within us. The Spirit of God is arousing us within. We're also feeling the birth pangs.

- *Romans 8:22-23 MSG*

Evolution testifies to a creation struggling and grasping to bring forth more than its past. Yet creation is inherently free to take turns and twists that are contrary to the nature and desire of God. The fall, in this context, is not falling from some pre-existing perfection, but falling short of what is possible. It is creating a narrative that is less than the love and beauty possible in God; it is choosing violence instead of transformation; it is building civilizations on the graves of victims, instead of embracing the outcasts; it is losing sight of the true image of God and therefore losing sight of our true nature and grasping after every delusion that promises fulfillment. Something better, more meaningful, and more beautiful is possible for us individually and for our societies collectively.

THE FALL RADICALLY REDEFINED

Is the concept of the fall still valid? The text most often referred to, in support of this concept - Genesis 2 and 3 - does not speak of a fall and does not even mention sin. The Old Testament is, in fact, oblivious to the later theological concept of a fall. It is only after the resurrection of Jesus that Paul searches for a comparison to this event that resets the trajectory of human development. In Romans 5 he compares Jesus to Adam but in the same breath admits that the comparison is inadequate. This passage would become the foundation for many interpretations of the fall. Especially an Augustinian misunderstanding of the text[2] (based on a wrong translation) would become one of the most influential interpretations of the fall. This popular idea of the fall implies, among other things, that a higher level of existence was previously a reality and that we have fallen from that state. Such an interpretation opens a lot of difficult questions: Why does God set up everything in such a way as to make the fall possible? Why invite humanity into an environment where this event seems inevitable? Why create the tree of the knowledge of good and bad if partaking of this tree is not something he wanted humans to do? And why not intervene if the consequences are so catastrophic?

This radically new understanding of the fall we are exploring here is also radical in the most fundamental meaning of the word, in that it returns to the root - the most original understanding of the concept. Instead of the image of a state of perfection from which we fell, the image of falling short - of not attaining the potential of our existence - is more appropriate to the Yahwist story. To state the same in a more positive frame: there remain possibilities of meaning, of beauty, of being, yet to be attained.

Irenaeus, one of the first Christian theologians, understood the story of Adam and Eve as one of human development that was stunted because of their impatience. Both the knowledge of good and evil and immortality would have been given to us, but through pre-mature grasping these human archetypes made the gift impossible. We can never possess divinity through grasping because it can only be received as pure grace. Irenaeus's stunning interpretation of these origin stories states that humans were destined to become gods! His insistence that it is a story of human development even goes as far as suggesting that both Adam and Eve were created as young children destined to grow and mature into a place where they could bear the fullness of divinity within themselves:

> God had the power at the beginning to grant perfection to man; but as the latter was only recently created, he could not possibly have received it, or even if he received it, could he have contained it, or containing it, could he have retained it.[3]

The implications of understanding Genesis as humanity's first archetypal narrative has profound implications for how we understand Jesus - the last Adam. Jesus retells the story of Adam but at each stage where Adam misunderstood and showed impatience, Jesus waits and learns obedience. In so doing, he undoes the archetype of the first Adam and introduces a new archetype, which is also the originally intended human - one who is free to receive all the possibilities of divinity.

> If it is haste that alienates human beings from God, insofar as it leaves them ill-disposed to receive divine life, a fitting salvation would have to undo this impatience. Christ also had to submit to time, to grow into perfection.[4]

Jesus recapitulates, summarizes the major points, in the human story and brings them to a radically new conclusion. As such, he reveals that the proper human relation towards God is one of waiting, of being open to the gradual unfolding of meaning. This posture is faith - not a presumptious confidence but a humble openness.

Central to the Genesis text is the creative processes that make us human, the relationships between God, humanity, and creation that converge in humans we recognize to be like ourselves. It is a story of divine seduction by which God lures humanity into the creative movement of becoming his image and likeness. But it is also a story that reflects reality - a reality in which humanity grasped for that which could only be received as a gift. Yes, we can say that a new concept of the fall is valid in the story, namely in the sense of lack, in the misunderstanding of God's nature, in the twisting of desire, in the impatience of grasping, and in the act of scapegoating others.

In this sense, the fall is not so much based on partaking of the tree of the knowledge of good and evil, but the means by which we partook. A parent might prohibit a young child from certain activities for their own protection. The two-year-old should probably not play with matches. However, at an appropriate age the child can be taught and trusted to make a fire. The prohibition against eating from the tree of the knowledge of good and evil can be understood in a similar way. To develop self-consciousness is not evil in itself, but is a creative process inspired by God. Imagining that we could remain in, or return to, a pre-conscious state with no knowledge of good and evil is to dream of being a two-year-old child forever. The capacity to make value judgments, to know degrees of good and evil is not a bad thing in itself. The process by which we get there needs transformation ... and I think that is exactly the kind of development of consciousness that Jesus introduces into this cosmic story. But again the simple capacity to know good and evil is described, by none less than God, as the capacity that makes humans like God (Genesis 3:22). The New Testament as well extols the mature virtue of being able to discern between good and evil: *"But solid food is for the mature, for those whose faculties have been trained by practice to distinguish good from evil"* (Hebrews 5:14 RSV).

UNFOLDING MEANING

The gospel is indeed larger than a promise of an original perfection restored. In this story, the beginning, no matter how beautiful and insightful it might be, does not contain the whole truth. Jesus introduces a whole new creation. And in this new creation, truth is not preserved in a legendary origin but continues to unfold in an ongoing narrative. As such the meaning continues to expand into a future that is not limited to the past.

There is very little room for ongoing participation in creation, if creation is seen as a completed past event. If there was a perfect blueprint of your design, and your only contribution was to discover that blueprint and live accordingly, then you have no creative contribution to make to your design! You can only discover who you are, you cannot participate in the creative process of becoming. The future becomes irrelevant, for the most it can contain is a repetition of that original perfection. Nothing is truly new. And so this philosophy remains stuck in a nostalgic attachment to the original – it has nothing more to offer, nothing new, no future. John Haught, in his book, *Resting on the Future*, opens up another possibility:

What would it imply theologically if we looked forward to the future transformation of the whole universe instead of trying to restore Eden, or yearning for a Platonic realm of perfection hovering eternally above the flow of time? What if ... theologians and teachers began to take more seriously the evolutionary understanding of life and the ongoing pilgrimage of the whole natural world? What if we realized that the cosmos, the earth, and humanity, rather than having wandered away from an original plenitude, are now and always invited toward the horizon of fuller being up ahead?[5]

What a beautiful possibility: a God that is not stubbornly trying to conform us back into an original mold, but inviting us into an open and expansive future in which we get to co-create what has never been before? To open ourselves to these possibilities we have to unshackle ourselves from the concepts that reduce us to mere spectators.

Endnotes

1   Keller, Catherine (2003-12-16). *The Face of the Deep: A Theology of Becoming.* Taylor and Francis.

2   Hart, D. and Hart, A. (2019). *Traditio Deformis* | David Bentley Hart. [online] First Things. Available at: https://www.firstthings.com/article/2015/05/traditio-deformis [Accessed 21 Aug. 2019].

3   *Against Heresies* IV.38.2

4   Jeff Vogel, *"The Haste of Sin, the Slowness of Salvation: An Interpretation of Irenaeus on the Fall and Redemption,"* Anglican Theological Review 89, no. 3 (2007), http://www.questia.com/read/1P3-1327235991/the-haste-of-sin-the-slowness-of-salvation-an-interpretation.

5   Haught, John F. *Resting on the Future: Catholic Theology for an Unfinished Universe.* New York: Bloomsbury, 2015.

CHAPTER EIGHT

Girard's Narrative Conversion

MIMETIC THEORY

The very essence of what makes an individual is a unique story. The heart of what forms our societies are narratives. Consequently, the deepest transformation of both individuals and societies is a narrative conversion. Nothing really changes until our narratives change. Salvation is so much more than a transaction to appease an offended deity. Rather, it is a revelation that changes the meaning of our symbols and subverts our stories.

One of the greatest contributions ever made to the understanding of how the human story began, developed, and found its culmination in Jesus Christ, was made by the literary critic, René Girard.

The scope of Girard's ideas are enormous. They explain everything from the process by which individual desires are mediated to the formation of civilizations; from the development of the symbolic consciousness to the nature of violence and the origins of religion. It was exactly because of the sweeping scope of *mimetic theory,* as it became known, that it was subjected to intense criticism. But, after decades of scrutiny, scholars from diverse areas increasingly began to appreciate the profound power of explanation these ideas possess. Anthropologists, philosophers, theologians, neurologists, and psychologists began to not only confirm the validity of mimetic theory but expand, refine, and apply it in their respective fields.[1]

ORIGIN MYTHS AND THE BIBLE

Our interest here is in Girard's understanding of origin myths and, subsequently, the unique way in which the biblical Scriptures take the human story forward. The overview presented below is therefore kept to the minimum necessary to show the connection between these myths and the development of the biblical narrative. A more comprehensive treatment of Girard can be found in my previous book, *Desire Found Me.*[2] The structure of this mimetic story is not only present in history but is a pattern recognizable in our personal lives. Are there blind spots in the way we understand ourselves? Do we construct and live within the illusion of our own personal myths?

Origin myths share a common structure. Chaos features early and prominently, then comes a creative act of violence that brings about a new order. We have only lightly touched on a few of these myths in Chapter 3 but, in them as well, it is the "noisy" children, the dissatisfied junior gods, or the outright rebellious workforce, that prompt the senior gods to take action. The action always involves violence and is seen as creative, for a new order follows this time of upheaval. Girard recognized that real historic events lie behind these stories. Real communities faced complete breakdown as unrestrained violence threatened to destroy everything. But a new form of violence, *sacred violence*, could contain the situation and restore the peace.

Mimetic Desire and Chaos

Girard's interpretation of the chaos is that it represents a real community in crisis. But what caused the chaos in these ancient communities in the first place? Exactly the same dynamics that cause conflict today. It begins on a small scale, with individual desire, and develops into broader rivalry. Conflict and violence naturally escalate. A community does not instantly go from peaceful co-existence to all-out conflict. There is a momentum that builds; individual rivalries grow into communal conflict.

How does desire cause conflict? Girard's understanding of mimetic desire shows that what is actually desired is the being of another. It is a sense of lack-of-being that makes the being of another attractive. The object of desire is secondary. Do any of these insights remind you of the Yahwist narrative in Genesis 3? It was the suggestion that Eve lacked the likeness of God that made the fruit so attractive. In addition, the suggestion that God desired this fruit for himself exclusively intensified the desire. The awakening of desire goes hand-in-hand with a sense of lack-of-being. The Yahwist's keen insight into the human condition saw this process of grasping for what we think we lack as fundamental to human development.

Advertising agencies understand this principle and so they use the most desirable models to present their products. They know that what their audience unconsciously wants is *to be* the model. If the model therefore desires an object, the object becomes desirable. To be the model is a goal not immediately attainable, but the next best option is to have what the model has. Desire is therefore mediated. It does not spontaneously erupt within a person; but rather desire is suggested to us as we observe what others want. This leads to the profound insight that desire does not originate in the self, on the contrary, self is created by desire.[3] It is the very distance created by desire that allows the sense of a separate self to emerge.

It's not difficult to see how mediated desire causes rivalry and escalates into violence. Especially seeing that both rivals begin with a sense of lack-of-being. Mirroring one another's desires leads to a situation where rivals are always reaching for the same object of desire. This reinforces the suspicion that the rival wants to withhold from me what I desire. And so, the conflict increases. We can see this play out on a micro level when two toddlers are left in a room with multiple toys. The first point of interest for each toddler will be the other toddler. The next most interesting object will be the toy closest to the other toddler. When the first reaches out for that toy, the second one will realize that it is the toy he always wanted, and war breaks out. This comical example is, unfortunately, an insight into human history.

> *You desire but do not have, so you kill. You covet but you cannot get what you want, so you quarrel and fight.*
>
> *- James 4:2 NIV*

We've seen how desire can become twisted into coveteousness. How does this desire for what belongs to another escalate into violence? We can all recognize a situation in which an argument becomes more and more heated. As insults fly and tempers rise, the initial cause of the argument is forgotten. What started it becomes irrelevant because the rival becomes the focus of the anger. The greater the rivalry, the more each rival becomes like the other. From the respective positions of each rival, the other is the absolute opposite of who they are but, in reality, the rivals are mirror images of each other. We fight, not because we are different, but because we are the same. The more intense the conflict, the more all parties are conformed to sameness. Every act of the rival confirms the worst suspicion and energizes a retaliation that is a mirror reflection of the initiating act. Those caught up in this cycle of rivalry perceive the rival's act as evil and their own act of retaliation as justified. The cycle of violence always blinds those who participate in it. In truth, both acts of violence are the same. Anger escalates, and as more people become involved, the energy within this cycle is multiplied. To express that anger becomes more urgent than to find a solution to the original problem. No one remembers the original problem for no one recognizes their own desire, rooted in their own sense of lack-of-being, as the energy source of the conflict. The obvious and only visible problem is the rival.

SCAPEGOATING

Primitive lawless communities were constantly under threat of annihilation because of unrestrained violence from within and without. When violence is met with violence, a momentum grows. What might have begun as a dispute between two families can soon draw whole communities into its cycle of enmity. And if there is no restraint placed on this cycle, it reaches a critical mass where all distinction disappears in a war of all against all.

Consequently, when ancient tribes encountered one another it often resulted in the annihilation of one or both tribes. This cycle of violence was repeated innumerable times and became deeply encoded in the human psyche. But all across the world a solution presented itself. Instead of unrestrained violence, a new form of violence was discovered that could bring an end to the senseless chaos. Instead of a war of all against all, a war of all against one - a single victim - was much more efficient, safe, and just as satisfying.

The insight of Genesis 3 is again so pointed. One of the most characteristic qualities of the emerging human is the tendency to blame others for the difficulty faced and the experience of guilt.

When tensions reached a boiling point within lawless communities, violence became a cathartic release. Such a release would either come through chaotic mindless violence or the single victim mechanism - scapegoating. Because this whole process is one of projecting anger and guilt, it is easy to once again divert the focus of the anger when a scapegoat is presented. The guilt of the scapegoat is confirmed by the anger of the mob, and those who are still able to discern the situation without being blinded by anger know that the survival of the community is more important than the innocence or guilt of the scapegoat. A consensus is reached and the victim is cast out or murdered. The myths hide this process, but it is exposed in the gospel of John when *"Caiaphas, who was high priest that year, spoke up, 'You know nothing at all! You do not realize that it is better for you that one man die for the people than that the whole nation perish'"* (John 11:49-50). Here is revealed what the myths hide, namely the innocence of the victim. The true motivation is the preservation of the community. And for that cause, the victim is sacrificed.

Sacred Awe

Why is this founding sacrifice sacred? Imagine that primal moment of the first communal murder. Blind rage subsides and, as if awakening from a slumber, we begin to see the body of our victim. This is a profound moment in the emergence of consciousness. The *Lamb slain from the foundation of this world* is the one who calls our consciousness into a deeper recognition. It is a moment of sacred awe, for two extreme contrasts confront us. The moment of slaughter is both abhorrent and beautiful. Abhorrent for the brutal violence against one of our own; beautiful for the redemption it brought to the community. The combination of fear, mystery, and peace bring about a new sense of the sacred. Coming face to face with one so much like us, who has suffered a horrific death, makes us question: Who or what is behind this? How can I avoid such a fate? What higher justice demanded this blood? And we ask these questions because we cannot bear the truth, namely: I am behind this violence! I killed! But this is an answer we are blind to, for it would drive us insane. And so, another answer is invented. Gods of retributive justice are created so that we do not have to bear the responsibility for such horror. This is where the human narrative became deeply twisted, where the evil of violence was hidden under the symbol of sacred sacrifice, and the voice of religion was invented to drone out the gentle voice of divine love.

When the violence of pack animals causes the death of another animal, it does not result in a sense of sacred awe but, most probably, in the consumption of the dead animal. Why would the effect be different in primitive humans? Genesis 2 gives us a clue into the development of human consciousness even before the first recorded act of violence. When Adam perceives the woman as flesh of his flesh and bone of his bone, it is a moment of unique recognition. Human consciousness recognizes self in another. Our awareness of likeness, and the sacred face-to-face intimacy we can participate in, highlight a development in consciousness that would make violence more meaningful as well.

The human story takes a dramatic turn towards violence in the event of sacrifice. Gods are born - invented to validate the "truth" of our account. These gods may be known by many different names, but any god that exists to authorize our order and our violence is nothing more than a projection of our own deceptive guilt. It is all just an elaborate scheme to suppress the truth. Jacob deceived his father, constructed a deceptive narrative, and a delusional identity. In so doing he alienated himself from his father, from his unconscious (brother) and, consequently, from himself. But these words keep on ringing: *Who are you my son?* This is where the human story falls short of what it is called to. Good and evil become confused, for it is obviously good to save our community but the means by which we do so is evil. We have grasped for a solution prematurely.

The immediate effect of this cathartic violence is peace. Magical peace! The radical change of a community on the brink of utter annihilation, of a community being consumed by the monster of chaos, now transformed into stillness and peace, is perceived as nothing less than divine intervention. This is the moment in which the scapegoat is slaughtered. It confirms both the guilt of the scapegoat and the divine sanction of the violence. In some cultures the scapegoat became revered as the divinely chosen one or as an actual god. Despite being guilty of crimes, the scapegoat also saves the community and magically overcomes the chaos that would have consumed them. This event becomes the very foundation of a new order of community. Consequently, many civilizations have an origin myth based on a founding death. For instance, the founding myth of Rome is the story of twin brothers, Remus and Romulus, in which the murder of Remus begins the new order of Rome.

In reality, it was the anger of the mob, a demon of their own creation, that was projected onto the scapegoat. And the violence done against the victim was a type of cathartic exorcism. The problem was never the scapegoat. The origin of the chaos was always the internal turmoil of individuals that culminated in the chaotic mob. If the truth about this process is recognized, the practice of scapegoating would no longer be effective. But it is exactly because of the blindness of the community that the process works so effectively.

RITUAL, RELIGION & LAW

The dramatic effect of the scapegoating mechanism to bring an end to uncontrolled violence became the basis for ritual. Whenever it seemed as if chaos was about to erupt again, there was an attempt to replay the same events that redeemed the community from chaos before. Because we did not know exactly what caused the magical peace, the steps that lead up to the sacrifice are repeated in ritual.

Before the writing of mythical origin stories, they were told in ritual. Some of these ancient rituals are still practiced today. These rituals re-enact the events that lead up to the sacrifice, the sacrifice itself, and the consequent peace. Because the actual causes of the chaos and the sacred peace following the sacrifice are hidden, the rituals differ as they lead up to the sacrifice, but in the act of sacrifice they are remarkably similar.

Ritual became a key ingredient of religion and law. The first recorded law codes are all concerned with limiting violence. Violence gave birth to religion and religion became a way of containing violence. The Ten Commandments seem to recognize the actual source of violence as covetousness - which is to desire what belongs to your neighbor. Girard's book, *Violence and the Sacred*, caused a stir because it shed light on the process of violence and its relation to religion. At the time, it was rather fashionable to blame religion for violence. Girard convincingly argued that it was not religion that caused violence, but violence that caused religion. Humans were violent before any religion or civilization came into existence. These institutions were formed, partly, to contain the problem of violence.

MYTH SUBVERTED

Once we recognize that real events are the basis of these myths, it becomes important to understand who wrote them, for our perspectives are always subjective.

It was the surviving community that first preserved the myth in ritual and later in writing. The newly established order that was birthed out of the chaos and redemptive sacrifice used myth to promote its legitimacy. With the exception of a few, which we will look at later, all such stories were told from the perspective of the victors, not the victims. It was precisely because the noisy voice of the victim was unbearable that they were killed - the victors did not want to hear that perspective. And death is the most convincing way in which to win an argument! The art of writing was also the exclusive domain of the elite and practiced within the courts of kings.

The sacred act of violence therefore was always portrayed as a heroic, necessary and completely justifiable act. The victim of this violence is always portrayed as deserving of this fate, or in some cases, as a self-sacrificing hero. But never is the actual act of sacred violence, or in religious terms, sacrifice, ever condemned.

The bias of the story shows that the myth not only seeks to reveal truth, but also to conceal truth. It does not seek to conceal truth consciously, for the authors most probably sincerely believed that they were justified in their actions. However, the gentle voice of truth still found utterance in what these myths tried to hide. That is, that an actual murder took place, and whether the victim was guilty or not was not that important. The actual motivation for the violence is the necessity to preserve the status quo, to secure the peace, to silence the "noisy workers."

Most of these origin myths therefore have blindspots, moments that they hide or quickly glance over, to justify the act of violence as sacred and necessary. The innocence of the community and guilt of the sacrificial victim are emphasized.

NARRATIVE CONVERSION

It was while Girard was writing *Mimesis, Desire and the Novel,* that something completely unexpected started happening in himself. Girard recognized that mediocre novels are nothing more than the author's blind attempt to justify him/herself. Great novels, however, include a type of conversion, an event in which the author recognizes his own hidden desires portrayed within the characters. This recognition leads to a new honesty that frees the authors from the chains of mediated desire. And so it results in a work of literature that is significantly different from what it was originally planned to be. The conversion of the author is mirrored in the novel. Does this sound familiar? A story that is open to new possibilities, to the influence of the unconscious results in something much richer.

Regarding the writing of *Mimesis, Desire and the Novel*, Girard noted: "*I started working on that book very much in the pure demystification mode: cynical, destructive, very much in the spirit of the atheistic intellectuals of that time.*"[4] But Girard too would come to recognize the mimetic nature of the desires that formed him. The conversion process he recognized within the novels he studied suddenly found a reflection in himself. In Cynthia Haven's biography of Girard, *Evolution of Desire*, she notes:

> His conversion began as he traveled along the cluttering old railway cars of the Pennsylvania Railroad, en route from Baltimore to Bryn Mawr for the class he taught every week. While reading and writing as he chugged along between the cities, he underwent what in today's clinical and somewhat prissy modern jargon are called 'altered states' - and they apparently continued with more or less intensity for several months. [5]

Up to this stage, Girard was rather proud of being a skeptic. But this conversion experience, which he later described as a type of understanding, could not be denied. Once you understand, you cannot simply go back to not understanding. This process that began in 1958 came to a crescendo the next year: "*Everything came to me at once in 1959. I felt that there was a sort of mass that I've penetrated into little by little ... I'm teasing out a single, extremely dense insight.*"[6]

Themes of mimetic desire, violence, sacrifice, and religion naturally drew Girard to the Bible also. Many of the themes and story structures were the same as in other origin myths, but there were very significant differences. At each of the stages of myth in which the truth is hidden, moments that are ignored or skipped over quickly, the Scriptures pause and specifically draw attention to.

Scripture, too, sees an act of violence as the foundation for civilization. It is Cain, the one who kills Abel, who becomes the founder of the first city. However, instead of justifying this act of violence as something Abel deserved, the story calls it out for what it is: murder. Cain is not innocent in this act. It is the twisting of desire into jealousy that motivates his violence. The theme of chaos is present too, but in Genesis 1 the chaos is not overcome by violence but by a new relationship between Elohim and chaos. It is through silent hovering developing into creative word, by speaking more and more distinction into existence, that a new order is created without resorting to violence.

Humanity in their infancy misinterpreted many of the experiences and signifiers. As human consciousness develops in relationship with Elohim, these ideas and experiences need to be re-interpreted. Desire, chaos, violence, sacrifice, religion, our sense of the sacred, God, and humanity need to find new meaning.

The Scriptural stories are by no means a complete and clear debunking of the myth of redemptive violence. Rather, it is "*a text in travail,*" as Girard called it. Sacrifice, even human sacrifice, is still revered in many of the biblical stories. Chaos is often still portrayed as an enemy that needs to be slaughtered. As such many elements of the myth are still present, but a persistent unfolding of truth is setting a new trajectory for these stories. They are starting to undo the misconceptions of the divine, of violence, and of human nature.

New Perspective

Part of the reason for this subversion of myth is the perspective from which these stories are told. Remember, most origin myths were the official version of the birth of a new civilization. They preserved the perspective of the victors - of the established order. Imagine what origin myths would sound like if victims told the story! The Hebrew Scriptures do exactly that - introduce a radically new perspective. These biblical stories have their origin in a people who are outcasts, slaves, and victims. It is a people delivered from slavery whose tales survive and become literature only when they are a freed people in a kingdom of their own. Again, not every story is told from this perspective, but it is generally true and part of the reason why the Bible is unique in the message it conveys. The biblical narrative does not simply reproduce the symbols and meanings of myth but progressively subverts them. And subversion requires an entering in, an intimate familiarity with the subject, so that it can be transformed from the inside out.

Gil Bailie wrote about an exchange between a group of theologians who met in his office to hear Girard for the first time. After Girard gave an initial introduction, one of the biblical scholars responded:

> "Professor Girard, what you've been saying is quite extraordinary. It almost appears, however, that you are suggesting that the revelatory power of biblical literature is categorically superior to that of all other literature. You are, after all, a Stanford professor; you're not saying that, are you?" René's one-word response was all the more striking for the momentary pause that preceded it: "Categorically," he replied. The impression one had was that

Girard was the only person in this room full of Biblical scholars who was willing to say such a thing.[7]

The mystery of human desire, the myth of redemptive violence, and the very fabric of civilization, are finally subverted in the drama of Jesus' life, death, and resurrection. Human history is repeated in the sequence of events in which conflict intensifies as the Jewish nation fights for its survival, and Rome relies on its trusted method of violence to rule. The tensions are eventually diffused as all rivalries meld together into a united voice of condemnation. Jesus becomes the chosen scapegoat. He enters into the heart of our myth by becoming the victim and from there he exposes the myth. The true God does not participate in our cycles of violence but calls us to transcend them. This God does not justify our violence but suffers it. This God does not demand violence but in the midst of suffering offers forgiveness. The principalities and powers are stripped bare - the principles by which we have governed and exercised power are shown to be founded upon a lie. Light finally shines on the practice of sacrifice in this event of the perfect sacrifice ... and the truth it reveals brings an end to violent sacrifice.

GIRARD AND IRENAEUS

Irenaeus of Lyons recognized the narrative parallels between Adam and Jesus. He described the story of Jesus as a reversal of the story of Adam with such beauty - a kind of theological poetry. Both Adam and Jesus had to grow into maturity. But where Adam is hasty, Jesus is patient; where Adam disobeyed, Jesus obeys; where Adam wanted closure, Jesus remains open to the unfolding of God's purposes.

Girard enriches these insights in showing how Jesus subverts the myths of redemptive violence that were told in the actual events of repetitive cycles of violence throughout human history, even before the story of Adam was transcribed. The Adam story is an illuminating summary of the many myths from many cultures, revealing the processes that make us human and the misunderstanding that causes us to blame and scapegoat others for what we cannot bear in ourselves. Whereas Irenaeus could only draw parallels between Adam and Jesus, Girard demonstrates that this is much more than a poetic literary invention. This drama unfolds in the history of every civilization as the turmoil of unfulfilled desires escalates into communal crisis. Unable to recognize our part in this crisis, we project guilt onto our scapegoats to justify our violence. The myth of redemptive violence has been told over and over again through many generations and in many various cultures. Jesus achieves a narrative reversal by entering the drama and exposing its flaws from within, thereby subverting our myths.

GIRARDIAN AND PSYCHOLOGICAL SYNERGIES

Girard's understanding of myth is sometimes seen as antagonistic to more psychological interpretations. And there are striking differences. However, these different perspectives could enrich one another.

We have looked earlier, from a psychological point of view, at how chaos can symbolize the unconscious. Girard, however, sees the mythic chaos as representing an actual community in crisis. There is an obvious difference in interpretation here. But if we look deeper, we'll see that they are connected. Girard himself would argue that it is mimetic desire and the turmoil within individual persons that escalate into a communal crisis. The chaotic crisis without is, in reality, a projection of the unresolved chaos within. These perspectives are synergetic. And, indeed, a growing number of psychologists are applying Girardian thought to their field and the results are beautiful.[8]

What the biblical stories suggest is a whole new perspective and relationship with the chaos. It is not violence that solves the problem of chaos but rather a transformation of desire. Instead of projecting our passions and frustration onto others, the work begins within ourselves. And just like Jacob, we may find that the realm of the chaotic unconscious could be the source of new meaning - that God is in this I, I did not know. These psychological insights do not contradict Girard's interpretations but enrich them.

Similarly, mimetic theory can enrich a psychological reading of Scripture. Some purely psychological readings of Scripture will recognize the archetypal symbols that are also present in myth and, consequently, assume that these symbols have the same meaning. A recognition of the development of these symbols and how they are subverted by the biblical narrative is often not appreciated. Without a subversion of the meaning of myth, its blind spots remain hidden. Scripture leads us to a place of understanding that transforms - a place of conversion.

The fact that the Scriptures have much in common with myth does not mean it is simply another version of the same story. Rather, this is a case of a lamb in wolve's clothing. The whole cycle of violence is exposed from the inside out. The lamb that was slain through every act of violence since the foundation of civilization, would allow the principalities and powers to do what they have always done, but this time the truth of their deception would be exposed.

The principles on which our societies have been built, the power by which they operated, once again consumed the powerless lamb. However, this time death swallowed more than it could stomach.

Endnotes

1 See for instance: Goodhart, Sandor, Jørgen Jørgensen, Tom Ryba, and James Williams. n.d. *For René Girard*.

2 Rabe, Andre. 2015. *Desire Found Me*. Andre Rabe Publishing.

3 Ibid. Chapter 2 and 3. Also see Oughourlian, Jean-Michel. 2010. *The Genesis Of Desire*. East Lansing: Michigan State University Press.

4 Williams, James, ed, *The Girard Reader*, New York: Crossroad, 1996, pg 283

5 Haven, Cynthia L. *Evolution of Desire: A Life of René Girard*. East Lansing (Mich.): Michigan State University Press, 2018. Kindle Edition. Location 2320

6 Ibid Location 2373

7 Chapter by Gil Bailie in *For René Girard: Essays in Friendship and in Truth*

8 see Garrels, Scott R. n.d. *Mimesis And Science; Rene Girard and Creative Mimesis*. 2016. LANHAM: LEXINGTON Books; Oughourlian, Jean-Michel. 1991. *The Puppet Of Desire*. Stanford, Calif.: Stanford University Press;

Oughourlian, Jean-Michel. n.d. *The Mimetic Brain*

164

CHAPTER NINE

New Creation

GOD UNFOLDING IN FLESH

In the symphony of creation, Jesus is both a crescendo that concludes what came before and the silence that precedes a new beginning. The significance of this event divided human history into a before and an after.

Those who knew him struggled to find language to express the astonishing grace, the overwhelming truth, and authenticity they experienced in him. After his death and resurrection, language had to be stretched to give a glimpse of what they encountered. He did not simply offer an alternative perspective. No. Somehow God himself was embodied in his person. How does one symbolize with language, an event so real?

John's gospel returns to the language of Genesis, to the beginning. The audience of this gospel were comprised of both Jews and Greeks and the word 'logos' had distinct meaning in both these cultures. For the Greeks it was the principle that sustained the cosmos in the midst of chaos. For the Jews it was the Word that was spoken by God to create and sustain all existence. John's gospel declares that what we grasped at in these concepts has become flesh and intimately personal in Jesus. In all that exists a deep logic is at work and he names this logic, incarnation. All of creation is incarnation. All things exist in him, for him and through him (John 1:1-2). Yet, creation did not recognize what was enfolded within it (verse10). But those who recognize and receive this truth, are given the opportunity to unfold what is enfolded in them - to manifest the God who continually gives birth to himself (verse 11-13). And in them this inner logic becomes flesh. The truth and grace of our existence are on display in the person of Jesus Christ.

> And the Word became flesh and dwelt among us, full of grace and truth; we have beheld his glory, glory as of the only Son from the Father... And from his fulness have we all received, grace upon grace.

> John 1:14-16 RSV

Jesus did not come to show us what we could never be! He reveals the true depth of flesh - that God is present in all existence. The unconscious memory of blissful union, that unfiltered experience prior to the formation of language, is revealed as real. Jesus is aware of this union and his expressed intention is for us to experience this same union (John 17:22). To perceive my being as the gratuitous gift of grace, as the continual outpouring of God-becoming-flesh, is an experience that cannot but overflow in the act of giving myself for others. In union with him we once again partake of this wholeness, experiencing our completeness in him (Col. 2:10).

THE HUMAN ARCHETYPE TRANSFORMED

Jesus brings an end to the old human archetype of the first Adam and creates a new human archetype - in him the old human story is concluded and the new true humanity is summarized. *"The first Adam became a living being; the last Adam became a life-giving spirit"* (1 Corinthians 15:45). The repetitive cycle of victims and victimizers switching places from generation to generation can finally be broken. The human story can break free from the curse of endless mimetic rivalry and find its true trajectory again. The movie is rewound and the narrative is reversed. In Jesus, God finds a human in whom the very essence of divinity can be embodied. Simultaneously, in Jesus, humanity finds a God fully at home within our existence. God has found a human in whom the story can be retold - the story of God and humanity; the story of creation and incarnation; the story in which you are included. Jesus does not simply provide an alternative story to that of the first Adam. He, in effect, becomes Adam, becomes the human archetype, in order to undo the human story and bring us back to a place from which we can start again.

As mentioned before, according to Irenaeus, God did not create the earthling perfect and complete to begin with, for the weight of such divine perfection would have been unbearable. Rather Adam had to grow into the capacity to receive, contain, and retain the divine nature.

God had the power at the beginning to grant perfection to man; but as the latter was only recently created, he could not possibly have received it, or even if he received it, could he have contained it, or containing it, could he have retained it [1]

The essence of Adam's error was the haste with which he grasped for a share in divine likeness. Our first archetype could not wait but wanted closure, completion, and certainty. And in this covetous act of taking, the gift was made impossible.

Jesus, in contrast, submits to time and reveals that expectant patience is the right relationship of man to God. Being open to the unfolding of divine possibilities is not only for a season but is forever the correct human orientation towards God. Patient expectation makes the gift possible again. For the very nature of God is possibility. According to Jesus, God is the one for whom all things are possible.[2] To be open to possibilities is therefore essential to partake of this divine nature. Where the first human archetype became impatient and grasped prematurely, Jesus does not grasp, does not allow a sense of lack to cause him to cling but empties himself so that he may receive (Phil 2:6).

Pierre Teilhard de Chardin beautifully expresses this theme of patience as follows:

> Above all, trust in the slow work of God.
> We are quite naturally impatient in everything
> to reach the end without delay.
> We should like to skip the intermediate stages.
> We are impatient of being on the way to something
> unknown, something new.
> And yet it is the law of all progress
> that it is made by passing through
> some stages of instability—
> and that it may take a very long time.

And so I think it is with you;
your ideas mature gradually—let them grow,
let them shape themselves, without undue haste.
Don't try to force them on,
as though you could be today what time
(that is to say, grace and circumstances
acting on your own good will)
will make of you tomorrow.

Only God could say what this new spirit
gradually forming within you will be.
Give Our Lord the benefit of believing
that his hand is leading you,
and accept the anxiety of feeling yourself
in suspense and incomplete.

The human story is being transformed in the very act of the mind of God becoming flesh. The way Jesus transforms our narrative is not by writing a critical review of our history but by entering the drama as one of the characters. The same events that played out in every generation would occur again in his life, but he will offer a radically *new interpretation* of these events. David Bentley Hart names this new interpretation, *a narrative reversal*:

> *It is because Christ's life effects a narrative reversal which unwinds the story of sin and death and reinaugurates the story God tells from before the foundation of the world - the story of the creation He wills, freely in his eternal counsels - that Christ's life effects an ontological restoration of creation's goodness.*[3]

Exactly how does he achieve this narrative reversal? Let's begin on a personal level by comparing the development of human consciousness, as personified in Adam and presented in the first section of this book, with Jesus' development.

JESUS AND STAGES OF CONSCIOUSNESS

Being fully human, Jesus developed through all the stages of consciousness as every other human. For our first human archetype, the emergence of self-consciousness went hand in hand with a sense of lack-of-being. What is different in Jesus' sense of self? As we saw in the Yahwist account, the experience of being alone is a prominent feature of the awakening of self-consciousness (Genesis 2:18). Consequently, God created a companion and it was in this reflective relationship that the earthlings continue to evolve.

It is in community that humans develop a sense of self. The bonds that develop between a baby and their primary caregiver will influence all future relationships. When we are left alone, with no one to reflect, our reflection turns inward. Rebekah's question begins to echo: "Why I?" Am I abandoned? How one interprets this experience of being alone will have a dramatic effect on one's sense of self and future connection with others. Attachment theory is a psychological examination of these early formative experiences.[4]

So, let me ask again, what is different in Jesus' development of self-consciousness? He experienced times of being alone just like every other human. And his *reinterpretation* of what it means to be human begins in these earliest experiences. That he was comfortable being on his own is implied in one of the only stories about his childhood. As a young child he was quite happy to spend days without his parents. For more than a day his parents did not notice his absence.

And the little child grew and became strong, being filled with wisdom, and the grace of God was upon him. And each year, at the feast of the Passover, his parents journeyed to Jerusalem. And when he had reached twelve years of age they went up for the feast as they were accustomed to do; And having finished their days there, and as they were on their way back, the boy Jesus remained in Jerusalem, and his parents were unaware he had done so. Rather, assuming him to be in the traveling party, they went on their way for a day, then sought him among their relatives and acquaintances, And, not finding him, they returned to Jerusalem looking for him. And it happened that, after three days, they found him in the Temple, sitting amid the teachers, both listening to them and posing them questions; And those listening to him were astonished at his intelligence and at his responses. And seeing him they were struck with wonder, and his mother said to him, "Child, why have you treated us thus? Look! Your father and I are in horrible distress seeking you." And he said to them, "Why did you seek me? Did you not know that it is necessary for me to be in the home of my Father?"

- Luke 2:40-49 DBH

This awareness of being at home with his Abba, even when his parents are not around, remains with him as he grows up. As an adult, when Jesus explicitly speaks about being alone, he gives us the key to his *interpretation* of such experiences. Jesus imagines God as a Father that is always with him. I do not use the word *imagine* to suggest that it is only a fantasy. Rather, he imaginatively participates in this unseen reality. And so Jesus' sense of self is profoundly shaped by his awareness of Abba.

"The hour is coming, indeed it has come, when you will be scattered, every man to his home, and will leave me alone; yet I am not alone, for the Father is with me."

- John 16:32

When there are no other people around and his reflection turns inward, he becomes aware of an Other within the self, just like Rebekah did. But in Jesus, this awareness of otherness within the self does not result in conflict and alienation but in a deep assurance of his Abba's presence. The connection between the conscious and the unconscious is not achieved after years of self-deception and conflict as in the case of Jacob and Esau. Rather for Jesus the heavens are open, and the ladder between this transcendent realm and his earthly existence is buzzing with activity. God is in this place - this I - and Jesus knows it.

And he said to him, "Truly, truly, I say to you, you will see heaven opened, and the angels of God ascending and descending upon the Son of man."

- John 1:51 RSV

JESUS, MIMESIS, AND SELF-CONSCIOUSNESS

The self, formed in this awareness of divine acceptance, does not need to compensate for a sense of lack-of-being through egotistical self-assurance. The type of certainty produced by self-assurance has nothing but its own testimony to stand on. Arrogance is always founded on the insecurity of having no other assurance except your own. But the assurance that comes from an understanding of the true relationship between self and God, produces a paradoxical confidence. For it acknowledges the nothingness of what it is in itself, and simultaneously the infinite source that sustains it. Living out of this assurance means a total denial of the certainty that is generated within oneself and a total dependence on what comes from another. Those who live from ego-centric confidence cannot understand this as demonstrated by their response to Jesus.

> Therefore the Jews started persecuting Jesus, because he was doing such things on the sabbath. But Jesus answered them, "My Father is still working, and I also am working." For this reason the Jews were seeking all the more to kill him, because he was not only breaking the sabbath, but was also calling God his own Father, thereby making himself equal to God.

> Jesus said to them, "Very truly, I tell you, the Son can do nothing on his own, but only what he sees the Father doing; for whatever the Father does, the Son does likewise. The Father loves the Son and shows him all that he himself is doing; and he will show him greater works than these, so that you will be astonished.

> - John 5:16-20 NRSV

The backstory to this exchange between the Jewish religious leaders and Jesus is an incident in which he healed a man on the Sabbath. He also instructed him to pick up his bed and walk, which was prohibited on the Sabbath. The religious leaders could not simply let it go, for what was at stake is the interpretation of Sabbath, God, and their culture. What kind of person could be part of a culture and yet have the confidence to so radically reinterpret it? Was he not, as all other humans, a reflective being, influenced by the people around him?

The basis for not working on the Sabbath was the fact that God rested from all his works on this day. However, through many arguments and theological discussions between the Jewish thinkers, it was acknowledged that although God rests he still maintains some essential works on the Sabbath.[5] Because babies are born and people die on the Sabbath, the work of giving life and judging the dead had to continue. In the Jewish understanding at this time, judgment followed immediately after death.

So Jesus answers them: *"My Father is still working, and I also am working."* *For this reason the Jews were seeking all the more to kill him, because he was not only breaking the sabbath, but was also calling God his own Father, thereby making himself equal to God.*

They could not argue with the statement that God is still working, but he was reinterpreting both the Sabbath and relationship to God. The fact that Jesus claimed to be imitating his Father, for them, meant that he was making himself equal to God! They could only understand such confident imitation as rivalry. In their perspective, Jesus sets himself up as an independent equal to God. But Jesus answers: *"Very truly, I tell you, the Son can do nothing on his own, but only what he sees the Father doing; for whatever the Father does, the Son does likewise."*

Jesus will have none of that egotistical self-confidence. He clarifies the fact that of himself, he can do nothing. His self was not formed in a sense of lack-of-being. Rather, his sense of self has *no being without God*, and therefore whatever being it does have is nothing less than the gracious self-giving of God. His sense of self is not an independent self, but it is one intertwined in the otherness of the God who sustains all things. He does not separate his self from a sense of union with God (17:21). Outside of this union, the self is indeed a limitation and a stumbling block. When we live for the preservation of the self, we lose what is most essential about us - the opportunity to give ourselves for the sake of another. "*He who finds his life will lose it, and he who loses his life for my sake will find it*" (Matthew 10:39).

And here we also witness the profound power of divine mimesis. Jesus does not achieve authenticity by denying his mimetic nature but by embracing it fully. His gaze is on humanity's true model - God - the one who's image and likeness define what it means to be truly human. In fully embracing our reflective nature, knowing that without God we have nothing to reflect except our own twisted insecurities, something truly amazing opens up. We begin to see the Father for who he truly is; he is not the one withholding as imagined in Genesis 3 but the one who loves us and shows us all things that he himself is doing. We can live in this place of astonishment!

> *The Father loves the Son and shows him all that he himself is doing; and he will show him greater works than these, so that you will be astonished.*

> *- John 5:20 NRSV*

Notice that the Father *shows*, not *tells*. If the Father tells us what to do and we listen, then we are obeying him. But the Father shows us what he is doing. The proper response to such a showing is imitation. And it is in the act of imitation that we are astonished to see the enormity of the work he can accomplish through us.

In conclusion, it is not a sense of lack-of-being that is predominant in Jesus' self-consciousness but rather a sense of the superabundance of God's self-giving love. Consequently, Jesus can say things like: "*All that the Father has is mine; therefore I said that he will take what is mine and declare it to you*" and "*the Father loves the Son, and has given all things into his hand*" (John 16:15 and 3:35).

The Mind of Christ

*Have this mind among yourselves, which is yours in Christ
Jesus, who, though he was in the form of God, did not count
equality with God a thing to be grasped, but emptied himself,
taking the form of a servant, being born in the likeness of men.
And being found in human form he humbled himself and became
obedient unto death, even death on a cross. Therefore God has
highly exalted him and bestowed on him the name which is
above every name.*

- Philippians 2:5-9 RSV

What is this mind-of-Christ that we are to appropriate? We have
seen how the twisting of desire is the basis for misunderstanding
God and ourselves in Genesis 3. This imagined god withholds what
we think we lack. The felt lack within produces impatient grasping
for what we are not able to bear. We grow up too quickly and in so
doing forfeit the gift.

But in Jesus we see what it looks like to be at home in the story,
to allow the unfolding of beauty without haste, to receive and give
rather than grasp and possess. Without the illusion of lack, there
is no opportunity for desire to be twisted. Beholding the favor of
his Abba eliminates any opportunity for a sense of inadequacy.
Gazing on this favor becomes the source of his sense of sonship,
of belonging, of approval. If my own existence is desired by God,
what room is left for a sense of lack? The story has been reversed!
The first archetype hastily tried to possess because of his sense of
lack. The final archetype pours himself out because of the overwhelming awareness of the inexhaustible gift of God poured into

his existence. Christ implanted within human consciousness a new way of being human.

All of creation is incarnation. The unconscious truth about creation is that every moment is made possible and sustained by the One who holds all things together. We are not excluded from this union but invited into the fullness of its bliss. Our memory of original wholeness is more than a nostalgic longing for the naive innocence we experienced before self-consciousness emerged, rather it is an inner drawing to once again acknowledge the depth of being, the presence of Christ.

HISTORY REINTERPRETED

It is not only the individual's narrative that is reversed by Christ, but the community's narrative as well. The collective consciousness of humanity needed healing just like individuals needed healing. Girard showed how similar events birthed similar myths. Let's now look at how Jesus enters this drama to unveil the hidden truth and open our eyes to the cycles of delusion we've been part of.

Tensions are high in the occupied territory in which he finds himself. Even among the Jews, many factions are escalating the conflict. Desires are raging. Frustrations find utterance in blaming. This is nothing new. The ancient cycle of redemptive violence is steadily building momentum. Someone is going to die.

When Jesus speaks of his own inevitable death in Matthew 23, he does not refer to it as a unique event but as something that has always happened. It is not the event of his crucifixion that is unique, but his interpretation of it! In him all these acts of scapegoating and the blood of victims will find new meaning - a new conclusion.

The actual logic at work in these events has been hidden since the foundation of this world, but Jesus comes to unveil these secrets (Matthew 13:35).

We have created our identities by negation, by who we are not, by opposition. Our tribes are formed by who we exclude. Civilizations are founded on the tombs of our victims. Like our archetypes, Adam and Eve, we have found someone to blame but never dealt with the turmoil within. We thanked God for victory over our demonic enemies and found some peace in the belief that God justifies our violence. But the things kept hidden since the foundation of this world were about to be revealed.

God enters the drama in a form of clarity never seen before, embodied in Jesus. He chooses his character - the outcast, the scapegoat, the victim. He takes us back to the very event that formed our sense of the sacred, the event in which we created gods to pacify our guilt and legitimate our order. This event is not only the founding event of our civilizations but also of the formation of our first archetype. Something went wrong with our story. In our haste for solutions, we closed ourselves off to possibilities. A fundamental misinterpretation took place that changed the trajectory of human history towards violence. Jesus brings us back to that formative event to uncover the truth and reset the trajectory of the human story. What actually happened? Who are the characters and what roles did they play in this founding murder?

Where and who is God in this act of sacred violence? He is the victim! He suffers our violence; he does not justify it. But ... this means the victim is innocent. And if the victim is innocent, the victor is guilty. Can't we find someone else to blame? Where's the Satan? Is he not the evil behind this tragic play?

SATAN REINTERPRETED

Scripture confirms that it is the event of the crucifixion that defeats the Devil (Heb. 2:14). How? Notice, the closer we move to the actual event, the less visible the character of Satan becomes. Is it because the very form of the satanic is transformed in the process of its exposure? Indeed, it is the exposure of evil that defeats it. The principalities and powers would not have crucified our Lord if they knew what was happening (1 Cor. 2:8). The very principles on which our societies are founded, the powers by which they rule, would be unveiled in this event. "*I see Satan fall like lightning*" (Luke 10:18). I see this mythical personification of evil exposed as the very earthly process of accusation and violent sacrifice. When we do not creatively deal with the chaos within, when we make no room for the spirit of Elohim to hover over us in silent contemplation, when we hastily blame others rather than patiently transform, then we project our turmoil. It becomes a monstrous other and so we contribute to this satanic cycle of violence. Jesus reinterprets the satanic as the cycle of accusation that leads to sacrifice.

Facing the crucified Jesus, we are made to realize that standing by while victims suffer, is an act of rejecting God. It is in this moment, when the full weight of our responsibility is felt, that God chooses to make his acceptance of us absolute. And Jesus said, "*Father, forgive them; for they know not what they do*" (Luke 23:34). Jesus demonstrates a God who does not get caught up in our cycles of retribution, who never enters into rivalry with us, but forgives.

Violence Reinterpreted

And so we come face to face with our own violence in the cross. It is in the act of violence where our story took a wrong turn; where we misidentified God and in so doing lost touch with our true selves. We had no patience to work through conflict, no appetite for conversing with our perceived enemies. But Jesus demonstrates a new way of being human and, consequently, a new way of being a society.

Why did Jesus have to suffer such a violent death? Why could he not pass away with a really bad cold and still have the same impact? Why the violence? By inventing gods who justify our violence we have become ever more callous towards it. Today, still, we outsource our violence to our governments and in so doing absolve ourselves of all responsibility. The centurion, who was present at the crucifixion, had seen many gruesome violent events like this before. He was a professional in the art of violence - unmoved, unfeeling, and fearless through years of practice. No doubt he found solace in the belief that he was only following orders, and the gods authorized those in command. The violence he witnessed inflicted upon Jesus was nothing unusual. But God opens his eyes: "*And when the centurion, who stood facing him, saw that he thus breathed his last, he said, 'Truly this man was the Son of God!'*" A new interpretation of human violence is given when we too, like the centurion, stand facing the crucified Christ. God does not justify our violence, he suffers it! God is present in our victims!

In the mythic stories, the sacrificial death of the victim brings the chaos to an end for a season. It could only be for a season, for sacrifice is a solution that only deals with the symptoms and not with the cause. However, in myth, this event marks the end of the story for the victim. But something truly new is about to unfold.

For these myths, so deeply encoded in human consciousness, to be subverted, a dramatic new event has to break the cycle.

RESURRECTION

The resurrection transforms the human story like no other event. For the first time we come face to face with our murdered victim. Before this event we consoled ourselves with the belief that the brutal death of our victims must have been the will of God. Otherwise, why would he allow it? But when Peter declares that the one *we* killed was raised up by God, it is obvious that God is not complicit in our act of murder. Stephan too, in his address to the religious leaders, makes it clear that Jesus was betrayed and murdered by humans. But God raised him up and honored him. It is Stephan's vision of Jesus at the right hand of God that is unbearable to those who hear him.

What is even more surprising is the message of the resurrected victim. The blood of all our victims prior to Christ called out for one thing - vengeance! But Jesus' blood speaks a better message than the blood of Abel (Heb. 12:24). Jesus breaks out of the cycle of retributive justice, offers forgiveness, and calls both victims and victimizers to repentance. We can understand why victimizers should repent, but why would victims need repentance? Because both have allowed themselves to be formed by violence. Even in resisting injustice, the victim too is formed by violence. The resurrected Jesus transcends both these categories and shows us what it means to be fully human. To resist rivalry and refuse to be defined by violence is essential in returning to the image and likeness of God.

Paradise Restored or New Creation?

In what way does the life, death, and resurrection of Jesus save us? Does he restore us to an original state of perfection? We have already established that there never was a historical state of perfection. At most, it was the pre-conscious experience of wholeness. And we cannot return to the pre-conscious condition in which we were enveloped in the whole. We cannot undo self-consciousness, neither should we desire to. Having no value system is not desirable. But most importantly, there is a depth of relationship that only happens between independent wills, a richness of intimacy that is only possible when the borders of distinct persons are crossed and they willingly intertwine. To lose that is to lose what makes us fully human.

The conscious self has introduced us to new experiences - loneliness, separation, value judgments, and death-consciousness, but also the intimacy possible between independent beings. The path forward is to bring these distinct parts of ourselves, conscious and unconscious, into new and meaningful relationship. Now that these distinct complexes have developed, new connections between them can also develop. The aim is therefore to nurture a relationship between the intuitive wisdom of the unconscious and the logical wisdom of the conscious. This is where the redemptive work of Christ becomes central. Where our first archetype stopped the creative process of becoming the image and likeness of God, Jesus, the new archetype, resets the process. Through him we may again enter the Eden of possibilities, the flow of becoming divine. Through Christ we can exit the state of grasping and enter a position of receiving.

The haste of sin is finally a desire for closure, a wish to be done with waiting, which can manifest itself as much in the decision to settle for far lower than what is intended for one as in a grasping after what is higher. The uniting factor in both cases is the desire no longer to be liable to the operation of another.[6]

If the essence of human error was the haste with which we sought to bring an end to uncertainty - the sense of lack that urged us to possess and the act in which we closed ourselves to the possibilities of divine gifts - then restoration is placing us back in that position where we may once again be open to divine possibilities. The salvation Christ offers is neither a restoration to a state of original perfection, nor an advance to the end of our journey, but a positioning in which the gift is possible again. It is partaking of the mind of Christ in which both the logic and creative novelty are operative. Divine logic is not the kind of certainty that closes us up to possibility. Neither is divine creativity the kind of imaginative spirituality that has no grounding in reason. The mind of Christ is both the sober insight into reality as it is and the joyful expectation that reality may be transformed.

Conclusion

Somewhere within human history, a turn was made towards violence. The narrative took a turn and its trajectory pointed towards futility. It became a boringly predictive dead-end story. The fear of death became the underlying anxiety that motivated the human drama. These cycles of self-preservation and violence were deeply embedded in our psyche. Adam is the personification of this history and if you are human it is part of your story. Today still, this narrative framework is the confinement within which many understand themselves and view the world.

When security becomes more important than the adventure, when the comfort of the familiar becomes more attractive than the thrill of the unknown, when we grasp for certainty at the expense of being astonished, and when we embrace an order so rigid that there is no space for bewilderment, then the same fallen narrative of the first Adam continues to imprison us. As our frameworks of interpretation become hardened, life becomes brittle and the inevitable takes the place of the possible.

Jesus models a new way of life, an openness to the God of possibility. His confidence is not in the correctness of his own desires or ideas, but in the assurance that comes from another. He discovers a source beyond himself. And it is in relationship with this Creator that his own creativity comes into its fullness. Union with God does not dissolve him but enables him to become more distinctly, truly, and freely himself. And this God-man union has surprising implications for God as well. God is not limited or reduced in this union but finds opportunity to love and exist fully and freely. Jesus is the archetype of this union. He is the realization of this ideal within human history.

God is excited about your life my friend! In you God sees an opportunity to live and move and have his being in a way that is absolutely unique. Nowhere else does he have the relationships he has in you. And what he offers is nothing less than the freedom and ability to co-create with him. Together, he anticipates a journey filled with astonishment, wonder, and beauty - a path with surprising obstacles and even more surprising and creative ways of navigating those obstacles.

Can you hear His whisper: "What beauty and meaning are possible for you? Something truly new is possible for you. *Bring forth life.*"

Endnotes

1   *Against Heresies* IV.38.2.

2   Matthew 19:26

3   Hart, David Bentley. *The Beauty of the Infinite: The Aesthetics of Christian Truth*. Grand Rapids, MI: William B. Eerdmans, 2004.

4   Cassidy, Jude, and Phillip R. Shaver. *Handbook of Attachment: Theory, Research, and Clinical Applications*. New York: The Guilford Press, 2018.

and

Regier, Michael, and Regier, Paula. Emotional Connection: *The Story & Science of Preventing Conflict & Creating Lifetime Love*. MPR Press (May 25, 2017)

5   see F.J Moloney, *Signs and Shadows*: Reading John 5-12. Minneapolis: Fortress Press, 1998

6   Jeff Vogel, "*The Haste of Sin, the Slowness of Salvation: An Interpretation of Irenaeus on the Fall and Redemption*," Anglican Theological Review 89, no. 3 (2007),

ADDITIONAL RESOURCES

Mimesis Academy Online School - https://www.mimesis.academy

An online program drawing from cutting-edge research in psychology, anthropology, philosophy and theology.

Many of the students who have completed this program describe the experience as an intellectual conversion. Others speak of transformation. What these comments reveal is that the outcome of this program aims to be more than simply confirming what you already believe. Rather, its aim is to unveil reality in a fresh way and enable individuals to re-orientate themselves around these new realities. Each of the programs below consists of 6 courses and runs from January to December.

Ministry website - https://alwaysloved.net

A list of books, albums and other resources can be found here.

CPSIA information can be obtained
at www.ICGtesting.com
Printed in the USA
FSHW020514310320
68655FS